HEARING FROM HEAVEN

A MEMOIR OF GOD AT WORK AT MOUNT HERMON

Roger E. Williams

FORWARD BY BILL BUTTERWORTH

MOUNT HERMON PRESS

CALIFORNIA

Published in 2014 by Mount Hermon Press

I have tried to recreate events, locales and conversations from my memories of
them. Some names and identifying details have been changed to protect the
privacy of individuals.

All Scripture quotations, unless otherwise indicated, are taken from the Holy
Bible, New International Version®, NIV®. Copyright © 1973, 1978, 1984, 2011 by
Biblica, Inc.™ Used by permission. All rights reserved worldwide.

Williams, Roger E.
Hearing from Heaven: A Memoir of God at Work at Mount Hermon
ISBN 978-0-9908887-0-3

Collaborator: Bill Butterworth
Editors: Lisa Olson, Karen O'Connor
Layout & Design: Josh Bootz
Production Manager: Murphy Felton

This book was composed in Chaparral Pro & Neutraface 2

Printed in California

10 9 8 7 6 5 4 3 2 1

Mount Hermon Press books are available at special discounts when purchased
in quantity, as well as for fundraising or educational use. For details contact:
press@mounthermon.org or the address below.

mount**hermon**
PRESS
PO Box 413, Mount Hermon, CA 95041
mounthermon.org

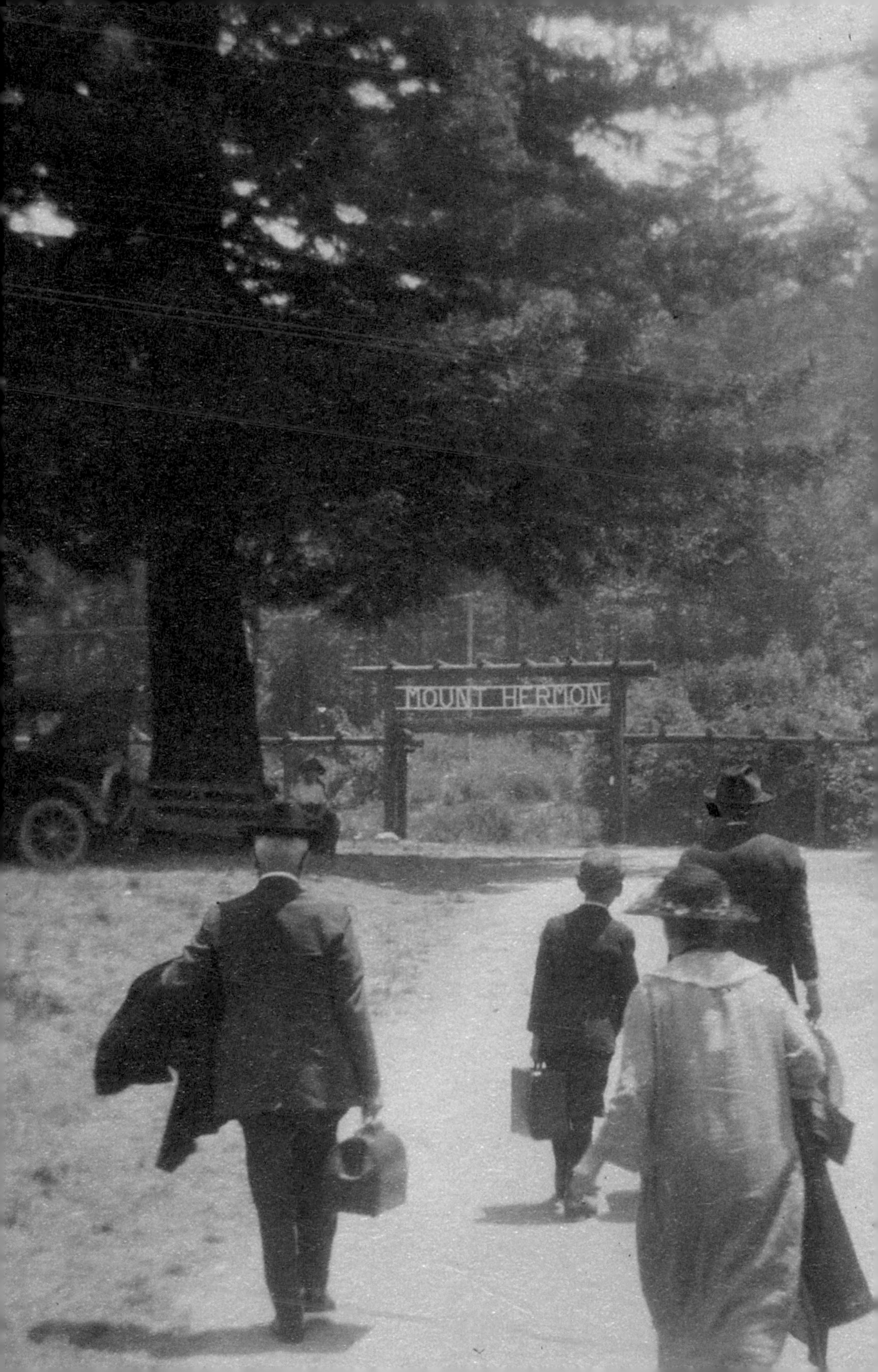
MOUNT HERMON

ABOUT THE AUTHOR

THIS BOOK IS PRESENTED IN LOVING MEMORY OF THE AUTHOR. It had cleared the final editorial review and was awaiting the final pieces of indexing, cover design, forwards and photo selection when Roger went to his heavenly home, far too soon for those who loved him, on Sunday, September 14, 2014 at 3:50 p.m. Roger succumbed to the cancer that he called "his insidious dance partner" after more than two years of arduous struggle during which he continued to teach, preach and provide visionary leadership for the ministry that he loved. His death came just a few days after his 21ST anniversary as President and Chief Executive Officer of Mount Hermon. He was 67 years young.

Roger is survived by his bride of 43 years, Rachel, and two daughters: Sara, wife of Jeremy Bentley and mother of Dylan and Luke, and Joy, wife of Nate Yetton and mother of Miles.

Having begun his professional career working in government and business, Roger took an abrupt turn from the fast track in 1981 to accept a call to ministry and began his career directing camps and conference centers. His legislative and business backgrounds enabled him to bring professionalism, an entrepreneurial spirit and unique perspective to this calling which has impacted not only the ministries he has led, but has also affected thousands of camp and conference centers nationwide. An ordained minister of the gospel, Roger served as pastor to many through his para-church leadership.

At Mount Hermon Roger's administration spanned the "dot-com" bust and the "great recession," with Mount Hermon continuing to thrive and have tremendous ministry impact through it all. His visionary leadership empowered his staff to pioneer outreach into non-traditional groups using ministry tools such as Outdoor Science School, the Redwood Canopy Tour and the soon-to-be-built Velocity Bike Park.

Known for his "superfluous verbiage," Roger enjoyed word play, puns, story-telling and banter, but never at someone else's expense. The master of the corny joke, his series of quips describing life are unforgettable to all who knew him. He embraced life with vigor and was "all in," all the time. He was a fanatical Giants fan, a meticulous craftsman with wood, a gourmet cook, a voracious reader of westerns, an advocate for Jeeps and Harleys, a North American big game sportsman and fisherman, a marathon finisher, and diligent student of the Bible. A prolific teacher and writer, his files include hundreds of sermons, seminars and articles that have deeply impacted many thousands of people all over the world. He celebrated and enjoyed people and was a great cheerleader in encouraging others to be who God created them to be. Above all, Roger loved to introduce people to a personal relationship with his Lord and Savior, Jesus Christ.

The Roger E. Williams Memorial Fund has been established with gifts directed to helping Mount Hermon achieve the envisioned future that Roger has articulated for those who follow. To contribute, visit *mounthermon.org/give*.

CONTENTS

FOREWORD

BY BILL BUTTERWORTH

"**B**Y THE WAY, MAY I JUST SAY, THANK YOU!**"** I can almost hear Roger's voice emanating out of the treasured plastic souvenir that stands guard on my office shelf. If I touch the top of it, even slightly, it enthusiastically nods in agreement with all I think or say. It is a Roger Williams Bobble Head.

Having known Roger Williams for more than twenty years, writing the Foreword to his memoir could subject a reader to piles and piles of wise, witty and wonderful anecdotes. Roger was a true Renaissance Man and stories of his life could fill an entire book (get it?!) In kindness to the reader, instead I will choose a single day in my relationship with Roger on which to focus. It's a day of rich celebration, affirmation and appreciation. Plus it's the date I was given the Bobble Head—August 28, 2013.

It was a Wednesday, a warm late summer evening in the quiet little town just south of the Bay Area that Roger called home for the last twenty years--Mount Hermon, California. Just a week before Roger and his lifelong soulmate, Rachel had team taught a workshop at Mount Hermon's Creating A Legacy Conference. Their topic creatively titled, "The Fine Art of Dancing With Porcupines,"

PREVIOUS Real Roger with Bobble Head Roger

was a look at personality differences in marriage. As usual, based on the evaluations, they clobbered the ball right out of the park.

Wednesday was an off day at the Conference Center, with a full summer of ministry successfully completed. Actually it was all but one conference yet to complete. Friday evening the Labor Day Conference would commence, with its normal sell-out crowd. But on this "off" Wednesday, a confederacy of Roger's favorite folks had conspired to throw him a party that was a full-on surprise to the unsuspecting fellow.

The surprise was a celebration in honor of twenty years of service as the Executive Director of the Mount Hermon Christian Conference Center. Roger began his Mount Hermon tour of duty all the way back on Labor Day weekend of 1993 and thus, a party was in order.

On one hand, anyone could throw a party—you know, buy those stupid-looking upside-down ice cream cone hats with the elastic choker, purchase a white on white sheet cake at the local grocery store, maybe use candles that can't be blown out to guarantee a laugh, and give the guy a gift card from Target. But we're not talking about just anyone throwing this shindig. No, the Mount Hermon staff party planners decided the evening would be best spent with a program they entitled *Roger's Rapturous Roast.*

The event was a black tie affair. Roger was told they were going out to dinner with their dear friends, Rob and Nancy Faisant, who would deliver the guest of honor to the local BBQ restaurant (Roger's favorite) where the Roast was to be held. Conveniently stashed in the trunk of Rob's car was a gown for Rachel and a tuxedo for Roger.

Roger was beyond surprised. He was flabbergasted. Dozens of friends had faithfully kept their mouths shut so that he had no idea this festive evening was going to take place. There may have been excitement in the air, but all one could smell was the divine fragrance of barbeque pork ribs, baked beans and potato salad.

Once the Guests of Honor were changed into their proper attire, we savored the scrumptious meal before the official program began. The couple looked radiant, Rachel in her sleeveless black gown and Roger in his black tux, red bow tie and red rose boutonnière. They reminded me of a bride and groom at their wedding reception, holding hands, head over heels in love with each other.

René Schlaepfer served as the Master of Ceremonies for the evening. As the empty dinner dishes were cleared away, the program got under way. One by one, René introduced those who would be the "Roasters" for the evening. Lisa Olson, one of the key coordinators of the event had passed along good advice to the Roasters in preparation for the evening. "Really good roasts should contain a good balance of humor, heart and honor," she had emailed in advance. "Roasts are just an irreverent tribute. Roasts should include anecdotes, or a story that captures the essence and character of Roger. Although, there are plenty of stories, please, please, please limit your time to what has been allotted."

That's exactly what took place. There was laughter. There were tears. There were moments of love, honor and compassion, mixed well with good-natured humor, hilarity and embarrassment. Rachel sang a solo, introduced as a serious operatic octavo, but before long she had us in stitches with her antics. Roger's two daughters, Sara and Joy, told of growing up with a dad who was not especially known for his ability to put together handsome clothing ensembles. But they loved him just the way he was. Robin, Randy and Jon Singley, longtime close family friends, shared stories that had become legendary, featuring their father, Ron Singley, for years Roger's very best friend. And they even made a spot for me to say a few words, and of course, I jumped at the opportunity.

There was so much I could have said that evening. Had the occasion called for a serious presentation, I had an outline all ready.

ROGER WILLIAMS
Gifted Communicator.
Gracious Leader.
Generous Friend,
Genuine Family Man
Grateful Servant of God.

As I looked over the outline, it was quite obvious it really wasn't the right kind of outline for a Roast, yet one word leaped off the page higher than any other. It was the word *grateful.*

"When I think about stories that reflect the life of Roger Williams," I began, "the first thing I think about it some favorite pet phrases I have heard Roger use throughout the years. The first one is the phrase *"By the way..."* The second one is *"May I just say..."* The third one is *"thank you."* These are often used together to create what a public speaker would call an "aside" which could also be called a

René Schlaepfer, Bill Butterworth, & Roger at the Roast

"sidebar" or even a "rabbit trail." For example, Roger might say, as he begins one of his summer seminar sessions, "Open your Bibles to Luke 15. By the way, may I just say, thank you."

The crowd nodded in enthusiastic agreement. They laughed as I cocked my head to one side, assuming a typical Roger Williams pose. At one point or another, all of us heard Rog utter these phrases together, bringing a smile to our souls with his humorous aside. But was that what it really was? Simply a humorous aside? The more I pondered his presentations, the less I saw it as a spontaneous sidebar and the more I saw it as an intentional interruption—a display of gratitude. And that better defines who Roger was. He was a man characterized by thanksgiving and gratitude. He was always going around, thanking people for their part, however big or small, in the life of Mount Hermon.

That night I ended my little speech with these words: "With gratitude Kathi and I commend you, Roger for your visionary leadership and your servant's heart. You are a Prince of a man serving the King of Kings. I love you and am honored to call you my friend."

And with that, I sat down and opened up the gift that each of us had placed at our table—our own personal Roger Williams Bobble Head.

That's the single day I choose to remember when I think back on more than twenty years with my dear friend. And that's why that Bobble Head speaks words of gratitude to me every time I look over at him on my shelf.

———— • • • ————

This book is a hybrid—part history of a ministry, part memoir of a man—all of it seen through the eyes of Roger Williams. For many of us who will read the following chapters, it's difficult to think of Mount Hermon without thinking of Roger Williams and it's difficult to think about Roger Williams without thinking of

Mount Hermon. The two seem melded together. Yet, as I write these words, my head is still spinning from a phone call sharing with me that Roger is no longer at Mount Hermon. He is in Heaven. He went Home to be with His Lord just a few hours ago.

Mount Hermon will go on and, not in small measure due to the tireless efforts of Roger Williams. Some will say its very best days are ahead.

So, Rog, by the way, may I just say, thank you.

Bill Butterworth
Newport Beach, CA
September 14, 2014

ONE

An Astonishing Prayer

*And they were all amazed at
the greatness of God.*

LUKE 9:43 (NIV)

"**I** CAN'T GO ANY FURTHER. Let's stop and pray."

Not necessarily unfamiliar words at a place like Mount Hermon Christian Camps and Conference Center. This ministry has been built and sustained by the fervent prayers of God's people for well over one hundred years.

No, it wasn't the words that were unfamiliar. It was the unusual *timing.*

The man who uttered those words was Bruce Wilkinson, founder of *Walk Thru the Bible* ministries and author of the bestselling book, *The Prayer of Jabez.* It was Family Camp 1, July 6-12, 1997, Bruce's first summer in years speaking at Mount Hermon Conference Center.

And there was nothing unusual about this particular week of Family Camp. The toddlers were in child care, children were at day camp, the teenagers attending youth meetings, and the adults in the auditorium. There were elective seminars, nature hikes, delicious donuts during the morning break, swimming at the pool, ice cream sundaes at the Snack Shop, crafts in the craft room, pancake breakfast up on the ridge, sports activities on the meadow, train day, vespers, Jack Pearson concerts by the campfire, s'mores, Book Shop browsing, Dad's Big Splash Contest, fabulous

PREVIOUS Kids arriving for Day Camp at the original Newton Memorial meals in the dining room, and Victory Circle followed by a closing celebration on the Commons. It was a regular week of summer Family Camp at Mount Hermon.

Our morning speaker was Bill Butterworth, and since it was family camp, he was speaking on the topic of parenting. Bruce was the evening presenter, challenging us in our spiritual walk with four messages from John 15 on the subject of bearing fruit.

This particular week had been the Christian Reformed Church Conference for well over sixty years. For 1997 they asked if we would help them book speakers and were excited when these two men accepted our invitation. We also agreed to program the week for them.

In my role as the Executive Director[1], I keep my ear to the ground for as much feedback as possible. Early in the week, I began to hear reports of God working in the hearts of our conferees. Bruce was on fire, and the Holy Spirit was at work.

Bruce's outline from John 15 included four different stages of fruit bearing:

- No Fruit
- Some Fruit
- Fruit
- Much Fruit

In between each stage he gave opportunity for an intentional step of growth and people responded. It was obvious God was using him to touch the lives of our guests.

Throughout the week many asked Bruce for private conversations and he cheerfully complied. It was a particularly busy week for me. Consequently, I didn't have any time to visit with Bruce except for Wednesday night when we invited him to our home for dessert. Since this was a regular occurrence for us, Rachel and I expected our two daughters, Sara and Joy, to join us with the speaker. After a reasonable length of time, the girls were free to politely excuse themselves and go on with their activities.

I will always remember that evening because our daughters were fascinated with their conversation with Bruce. Right out of the chute he asked them, "What is the Lord saying to you these days?" They found that question intriguing and started speaking from their hearts. They talked with Bruce for well over *two hours*—because they wanted to! As a result, I didn't get much time to interact with him that night, but was pleased Sara and Joy wanted to learn from him.

Sometime during that week Bruce shared a very personal experience from the platform. "You know *Walk Thru the Bible* started right out here on a bench in the Commons." He explained that, years ago, while teaching at Multnomah School of the Bible, God began talking to him about starting a ministry that would help others really understand the Bible. "I remember my wife thought I was crazy," he added with a chuckle.

Bruce Wilkinson in 1996

During that same summer he spoke at Mount Hermon about what God was stirring him to do. Between sessions a farmer from California's Central Valley came up to him and asked if they could talk, and they sat down on a bench in the Commons.

"Bruce, you shared your vision today and I want you to know one of the reasons God had you do it."

"Why?" Bruce asked.

"Because He told me before I came this week to bring some money along for a *special purpose*. Now I realize your vision is that special purpose, so here—this is for you." And he handed Bruce a large brown paper bag, adding, "God told me to bring cash."

When Bruce opened the bag his eyes widened. It contained *THIRTY THOUSAND DOLLARS!*

"You're the reason God led me here," the man concluded humbly.

Bruce never forgot that moment and it would play into what happened next.

———— • • • ————

My wife, Rachel, was excited to attend Bruce's Thursday evening session. Unfortunately, I was involved off-site in a community board meeting. I had no idea what I missed until I returned later that night.

Arriving back on campus, I parked my car in front of Forest Hall in order to run into my office to pick up some paperwork I had neglected to bring home. While walking to the Administration Building, two men who were long time Mount Hermon constituents, approached me. There was no question they were not happy campers!

"What happened tonight was so out of character for the ministry of Mount Hermon. Why did you put Bruce up to it, Roger? What were you thinking? It was totally inappropriate," said one.

Incredulous, I asked what they were talking about.

"It was manipulation, pure and simple," the other replied. "This is not how God works."

Once they calmed down I picked up bits and pieces of what actually occurred. I admit I was surprised if what they reported was truly what had taken place. As I listened to them, the Lord gave me words to say. "Men, who are we to say God can only work in certain ways? Is He bound by only what's familiar to us? If this is from God we're going to witness a miracle tomorrow. If it's not from Him, we'll see it fall flat on its face. We need to allow God to be God."

Then I drove straight home, sat Rachel down, and asked her to give me a blow-by-blow account of all that transpired that evening.

"Everything went pretty much the way it always does," she said. "After a time of worship, Dave Neely (our Director of Advancement at the time) stood up and explained that tomorrow morning we will be taking our one offering for the week. It was specifically earmarked for the construction of our new Day Camp Building. He explained that the current building was erected in 1931 to accommodate eighty kids and we currently have more than two hundred kids using the facility."

"Okay," I interjected, "that all sounds pretty normal."

"Exactly," Rach agreed. "And then Bruce got up to speak...He introduced his topic for tonight and was five or ten minutes into his message when he suddenly said, 'I can't go any further. God is speaking boldly to me right now and I can't preach anymore until I share what He is saying.'"

Motionless, I waited to hear more.

"Bruce turned to Dave Neely sitting on the front row and asked, 'Dave, what is Mount Hermon's greatest financial need?' Dave answered, 'The new Day Camp building.' Bruce asked, 'How much will it cost to build the Day Camp building?' Dave seemed a little surprised by that question. 'Our best estimate is around 2.5 million dollars.'

"'And how much do you have right now in the Building Fund?'

"'Six hundred thousand dollars,' Dave replied.

"Bruce turned back towards the crowd. 'Tomorrow we'll take an offering. I want you to break up into groups of three or four and pray. Let's pray specifically that God will bring in 1.9 million dollars in tomorrow's offering.'"

Rachel continued. "Everyone seemed shocked. It was deathly quiet! Bruce went on to say, 'When a ministry has been fruitful in your life, we need to be prepared to help support it. Mount Hermon has been fruitful in my life so I need to give back to this ministry. I can assure you I will be a part of the giving tomorrow.'"

"Wow!" I didn't know what else to say.

"There's *more!*" Rachel explained.

"More?"

"Yes. We broke into small groups and began to pray. At first it was awkward, but before long there was a clear sense of God's presence. Suddenly, Bruce interrupted us and said loudly, 'STOP!' We all looked up from our prayer groups to see what was happening.

"'The Lord just told me there is someone in this auditorium through whom God wants to give Mount Hermon one million dollars. I don't know who that is. Let's pray for that one person that God will give him or her the courage to be obedient.'

"We continued to pray," Rach added. "At the same time I tried to listen to what was occurring all over the auditorium. I heard the word million. I got goosebumps!"

"I can only imagine," I replied.

"Once we finished praying, Bruce returned to the platform and said, 'Now I can finish my message.' And he did."

All I could say was, "Amazing!"

"This is going to be a great day Roger! I'm so excited to see the Lord's power..."

I went to bed that night realizing the next day could be one of exhilaration as we experienced a demonstration of God's power, or I was going to be listening to a lot of disgruntled people scolding me for bringing in someone who would do what Bruce had done. I had never seen the gauntlet thrown down so boldly. I fell asleep praying for a miracle, but in my feeble humanity, quietly rehearsing my response in case it didn't happen.

The next morning I drove down to the parking lot behind the Administration Building, jumped out of the car and walked down the hill toward the Dining Room. Almost immediately a long-time Mount Hermon supporter approached me. At eighty years of age, Evie Nichols was more spry than most people half her age, but even so, I was astounded to see her *skipping* toward me.

Early Day Campers

to find Dave holding something in his hand. It wasn't a check—it was a piece of notepaper, ripped from a spiral notebook.

He had no words. He was sobbing as he handed me the paper. I read the following words:

> *July 11, 1997*
>
> *Guess this is an IOU. We can't write a check for a million dollars, but we can get that much out of our investment fund, and plan to do so. We'll send it to you within 10 days. We'd like this to be an anonymous gift. We've loved Mount Hermon for years, and are glad God used Bruce to motivate us to do something we'd never have thought to do ourselves. May the Lord always watch over this place in a special way and use it to change lives for His glory!*

A signature was scribbled at the bottom.

I attempted to compose myself. "Isn't this incredible? God has answered the million dollar prayer!"

Dave nodded and continued to weep.

When the total offering was counted, God's people had sacrificially given $1.55 million in that one Friday morning offering, just shy of the $1.9 we had prayed for! Adding the offering to the $600,000 already in hand, we had $2.15 million for the day camp building. We had estimated the cost for the project to be $2.5 million. In reality, when the plans for the Day Camp building were completed, the contactor's estimate on the final cost came in at $2.15 million. And he knew nothing about what we had in the bank for that new structure. But God knew exactly what we needed and provided. Our urgently needed day camp building was completely paid for before we ever got a brochure printed or launched a campaign. Awesome!

As I look back on that amazing event in Mount Hermon's history, it reminds me that God chooses to bless the genuine, fervent prayers of His "kids" as we authentically trust Him. Trust Him for the needed resources, and trust Him for His unique timing. He could have sent the money over many months, or quickly, as He did on this particular occasion.

In the months leading up to this miraculous offering, our Board of Directors had been weighing the best course of action in its desire to build a desperately needed new building for our day campers. Should we move ahead on construction by borrowing

1998 Newton Memorial construction funded and underway

funds? Or, should we commit this matter to prayer and trust the resources and timing to the Lord, holding back until He provided the funds? For years, the Board had borrowed funds on a number of new structures needed at the conference center, and the repayment of the loan often took years to liquidate. In these meetings, I challenged the Board to consider an alternative strategy: Pray and complete plans, but stay put until the needed funds are in hand so that when the building is completed and the first light switch turned on, the structure would be debt-free. What I like about this prayer and trusting strategy—not rushing ahead by borrowing construction funds—is that it allows God to be God. If He wants our project to be completed quickly, He certainly can marshal the resources to do that. If He wants it to proceed on a slower trajectory, He can do that too—or even prevent it. It allows Him to be sovereign.

Kids in Day Camp in 1998

We often say, "Mount Hermon is the Lord's ministry." This strategy confirms it. And when a project is completed, He gets all the glory. So after months of processing this issue, the Board decided to try this new approach with the Day Camp building. And then God took control, demonstrated His power and provision in ways we could never have asked for or imagined.

The end result of the Day Camp miracle funding was our Board making this strategy the new standing policy for Mount Hermon. Today we won't begin construction on any new major structure until 80% of the funds are in hand or promised in written commitments. Why 80%? Because in the time needed for plans to be approved by our local government, and the construction to be completed, experience has shown that the Lord will provide the remaining funds.

We talk of this as if it is a new strategy. But it really isn't. It's the way God has provided for Mount Hermon all through the years. It's the historic way God has chosen to bless Mount Hermon—His people pray, let go of their own agendas, and *trust God in the dark*.

Exactly how it all began, way back in 1905.

TWO

Go On In The Dark, Trusting God

*Who among you fears the LORD and obeys
the word of his servant? Let the one who
walks in the dark, who has no light, trust in
the name of the LORD and rely on their God.*

ISAIAH 50:10 (NIV)

I T WAS THE GILDED AGE IN AMERICAN HISTORY. The beginning of the twentieth century had a certain charm and innocence that leaves those of us who love history fascinated, perhaps even a bit envious.

William McKinley, the Republican Governor of Ohio, became President of the United States in 1897, ringing in the new century accompanied by his lesser-known Vice President, young Theodore ("Teddy") Roosevelt, former Governor of New York. Many felt Teddy was placed in the Vice Presidential role as a favor to the Republican bosses in New York; he was making too many waves in the Empire State. "Tuck Teddy away in the Vice Presidency so he won't cause any additional trouble," the bosses seemed to suggest by their actions, smug in their decision until McKinley was assassinated in September of 1901.

Roosevelt occupied the White House for the following eight years and would spark a world of new inventions, new industrialization, new conquests, and new endeavors. During Roosevelt's second term an historic event occurred which would impact all of the San Francisco Bay Area in general, and the beginnings of Mount Hermon in particular.

PREVIOUS Dr. Hugh W. Gilchrist (right) & Thorton Mills at Glenwood in 1905

One of the central characters in the early history of Mount Hermon was Dr. Hugh W. Gilchrist. Slender, with closely cropped, neatly combed dark hair, kind eyes and a warm smile, Hugh was born in 1858 with his roots in Indiana and Ohio. His father was an itinerant circuit preacher, traveling on horseback to minister to small groups of believers throughout the Midwest countryside.

But there were few "gilded days" for Hugh. His life was heavy with stark reality. When he was only four years old, his father died from complications of pneumonia as a result of crossing a stream on horseback riding his circuit. As Hugh grew up, he took on carpentry jobs and worked at a sawmill to help support the family. Eventually he attended Hanover College in Hanover, Indiana, graduating in 1885, and then Lane Seminary in Cincinnati, Ohio, graduating in 1888.

After graduation, Hugh was invited to pastor the famous First Presbyterian Church of Cincinnati and ministered there for five years. Then the Lord led the family to Gettysburg, Pennsylvania where Hugh pastored for three years, but it was soon evident God had yet another move in store for the young man and his family. They were to head west to serve Westminster Presbyterian Church in Seattle, Washington.

In an interview many years later, Hugh's son, Francis, gave us a glimpse of what life was like in the Pacific Northwest during those days:

> *When men, broken in spirit and often in body, flooded back from the Klondike gold rush, the church sponsored a hall in downtown Seattle for the purpose of helping to rehabilitate them. One of my earliest memories is of the rows of beds in that great dormitory. In this church my father was surrounded by a strong group of laymen with whose support aggressive evangelism was carried on in that pioneer city.*[1]

While in Seattle, an invitation arrived on Pastor Gilchrist's desk asking for his involvement in an event described as an "Assembly for Bible Study." It was to be held at a place called Ellisport, located on beautiful Vashon Island southwest of downtown Seattle, across Puget Sound. Dr. Gilchrist accepted the invitation and enjoyed a wonderful time of physical, emotional, and spiritual refreshment during the week. In fact, he enjoyed it so much he returned the following summer in 1901.

In that same year, Dr. Gilchrist received an invitation to join the faculty at San Francisco Theological Seminary. He was so impacted by the summer conferences he had attended on Vashon Island he told the seminary staff he would join the faculty if they would agree to hold Bible conferences "for the benefit of home missionaries and other Christian workers." The powers-that-be agreed and Gilchrist moved to San Francisco, bringing with him an idea that would smolder and eventually burst into flame. Dr. Gilchrist wrote to a friend about his vision:

> *Three such conferences were held at the Seminary in October 1902, 1903, and 1904. It was apparent that a mid-summer conference would be a better time, and a vacation place a better location.* [2]

And that's how it happened that a seven-day conference was held the summer of 1905 at Glenwood, California, only seven miles north of present day Mount Hermon. As might be expected, Dr. Gilchrist was one of the speakers and it was there he met Rev. Thornton Mills, a man with an engaging smile, pastor of the Second Presbyterian Church in San Jose, California. Both Gilchrist and Mills quickly discovered they shared the same vision for a conference center in this part of the country and began talking with conferees, displaying their excitement, and actually building into the schedule an hour each morning to discuss the topic, "Does the Pacific Coast Need a Western Winona/Northfield MA?" (Winona Lake was an established conference center in Indiana that had deeply impacted Dr. Gilchrist. Northfield, Massachusetts, was the location of a conference center called Mount Hermon established by the great Christian voice of the day, Dwight L. Moody.)

Rev. W.E. Crouser, who later became President and a Trustee of Mount Hermon, attended that first conference at Glenwood. In a letter he wrote in 1951, some 46 years later, he stated the following:

> I was present at the first meeting in Glenwood and heard Dr. Sherman preach a sermon that is still fresh in my memory. His text was 'Where the Word is King, There is Power' (Ecclesiastes 8:4). He said, 'Jesus is a King; we have His Word; therefore we have authority to go ahead; the power is ours, what are we waiting for?'[3]

At the end of the conference a vote was taken. "Do we need a conference center on the Pacific Coast?" The answer was a unanimous "YES!" There was nothing left to do but create a "special retreat for prayer."

The responsibility to move this vision forward fell on the shoulders of three faithful Christian leaders, Dr. Gilchrist, Rev. Mills and Rev. Henry Sanborne, another one of the speakers that week at Glenwood. In September of 1905 the three met at the old Occidental Hotel in San Francisco, with the bulk of the meeting spent in fervent prayer. Together they were convinced to press on with the vision.

A larger committee of people came together for the purpose of finding a suitable location for this new conference center. With the assistance of the Southern Pacific Railroad, the group traveled up and down the California coast, going no farther than two hundred miles from San Francisco on the coast and no farther inland than Yosemite.

They seriously looked at a location south of Carmel called Point Lobos, as well as back at Glenwood. Point Lobos didn't make the cut, nor did Glenwood. Interestingly, Glenwood was eliminated because the committee thought it was too small and lacked sufficient water supply for the size conference grounds they envisioned—Mount Hermon was obviously a God-sized dream!

Several on the committee were drawn to the Elim Grove of Redwoods on the Russian River, about two or three miles from Cazadero, but this property was eventually eliminated from consideration as well.

Then two large adjoining parcels of land in the redwoods of Santa Cruz County rose above all the others. The landscape was beautiful—no question there—water supply abundant, and to top it off, there were existing structures in place that could be immediately used for conference ministry. The lower parcel had a two-story hotel known as the Hotel Tuxedo, a bowling alley, guest cottages, and train station along with several other structures, so the committee started referring to that parcel as the Tuxedo Property. The other parcel included Arcadia Creek and was owned

by the Arcadia Development Company. It became known as the Arcadia Property.

With the committee now in agreement on property, there were important organizational issues to be addressed. An association was formed with the intent of selling capital stock to raise funds for the purchase of the land. But before they could sell stock, they needed a name. Dr. Gilchrist sheds light on this fascinating and God-ordained process:

> *The time came when the new enterprise must be incorporated and a name given to it. What should it be called? I took down my old Oxford Bible and studied the 460 names in Bible lands. Then I got a postal directory and went through all the names in the states of New York and Washington. To these were added several of our own choice or invention...*[4]

Because Pastor Gilchrist had been impacted by conferences in the east as a young man, he was aware D. L. Moody's conference on the east coast was called Mount Hermon. He sent a letter to the Moody family inquiring whether there would be any objection to

Mount Hermon in 1907 with Hotel Tuxedo at the edge of the meadow

using the same name for our conference center. Not too long after, a reply arrived from Moody's son, Will, who responded enthusiastically that they would be pleased if there was a "Mount Hermon of the West." So the name Mount Hermon was added to the list.

Stock certificate No. 734

...Sixteen names were placed in the hands of five Christian women with the request that they should add any other names they might desire, then from the whole number select a first, a second, and a third choice and return the same to the board. Four of them chose 'Mount Hermon' as first choice. All of them chose 'Glen Alpine' as second choice...When asked why they chose 'Mount Hermon,' the ladies replied, 'Mount Hermon is the reputed place in Palestine where Jesus went apart with His disciples and was transfigured before them' (Matthew 17: 1,2). Hence this name for our place apart with Him.[5]

With property selected, the name chosen, the next step was to draw up Articles of Incorporation, appoint a Board of Directors and ultimately acquire official approval from the State of California. Fifteen men from the original committee were appointed (along with sixteen others) to become Mount Hermon's first Board. They signed their names to documents on December 12, 1905, which were in turn notarized on the thirteenth and filed with the County on the fourteenth.

On December 26TH the newly formed Board gathered at the Hotel St. James to adopt the by-laws. Dr. Gilchrist was appointed Mount Hermon's "General Manager," the equivalent position I hold today as President/CEO. Rev. Mills was elected President of the Board.

It had already been decided Mount Hermon Association would offer stock to raise money to purchase the property. Those wishing to support the new ministry endeavor could do so. Stock offerings began in earnest as 1905 gave way to 1906.

By April 2, 1906 the Association had sold $30,000 worth of stock to two hundred eighty individuals. Approximately $13,000 was in hand and $17,000 in the form of promises to be paid later. On April 14TH, the Board confidently went forward with the purchase of the four-hundred acres, including the Hotel Tuxedo and accompanying structures, for the negotiated price of $44,000, trusting the $31,000 still owed would be covered by the $17,000 in written promises and additional stock sales.

It was a spiritually invigorating time—the vision of this ministry was so close to becoming a reality. The beginning of the summer conference program was only a few months away. How exciting to watch the Lord provide as His children fervently prayed. God was at work!

> *"It was a spiritually invigorating time—the vision of this ministry was so close to becoming a reality."*

Who could have known that at approximately 5:12 a.m. on April 18, 1906, only four days after that first payment was made, much of the Bay Area would be decimated by what would become known historically as The Great San Francisco Earthquake. The magnitude of the earthquake has been estimated at 7.9 on the Richter Scale. The epicenter was two miles from the center of San Francisco, but it was felt as far north as Oregon and as far south as Los Angeles. It even shook central Nevada. The quake and resulting fires were responsible for hundreds, if not thousands of deaths. To place it in a more contemporary perspective, that 1906 earthquake had as great an economic impact on the Bay Area as Hurricane Katrina did on the greater New Orleans area in 2005. It would test the mettle of the new Mount Hermon Association significantly.

At face value, it was a horrible time to be raising money in greater San Francisco. People suddenly needed every penny just to survive. So desperate was the situation, many individuals who had given money to Mount Hermon asked for part or all of their funds to be returned in order to cover their own losses. Others who had promised to buy stock, but had not yet done so, asked to be relieved of any further obligation.

The magnitude of The Great San Francisco Earthquake

This was a crisis of colossal magnitude. Mount Hermon needed the money to move ahead with the agreed purchase of the land parcels but those who had previously been so eager to assist were now drowning in their own financial needs. The Board members wrestled with this dilemma for over a month and then called a meeting for earnest prayer. While we don't have any records indicating the perspectives and emotions of these men as they entered this meeting, one can only imagine they were considering serious questions. Was the earthquake God's way of communicating His will? Did the Lord want them to slow down their plans for some reason? Or abandon them? How could they survive financially when all available resources were needed to assist in the rebuilding of homes and businesses in the Bay area? While we don't know their convictions as they entered the time of prayer, we do know the result. They clearly "heard from Heaven" during the time on their knees. Dr. Gilchrist fills in the details:

> On the last night of May 1906, we met at the old
> Y.M.C.A. building in San Jose to decide whether we should
> venture to go on or not. Our decision was 'God was in
> this before the earthquake, and He will be in it after the
> earthquake. We will go on. The need of the true teaching of

the Word is as great now as before the disaster. **We will go on in the dark, trusting God**' *(emphases added).*[6]

The faith and vision of the founders of Mount Hermon, and the willingness to trust God in the face of daunting challenges set the pattern for the future. Since then, myriads of other leaders in Mount Hermon's history have followed in their footsteps helping Mount Hermon become one of the largest Christian camp and conference centers in the world. Mount Hermon is an independent non-profit corporation governed by a dedicated Board of Directors, interdenominational in scope, evangelical to its core, and growing

The Founders of Mount Hermon

in its Gospel-centered outreach in proclaiming Jesus.

Today, we minister to more than 70,000 guests each year on one or more of our campuses. In the next fifteen years, we trust—with the Lord's help—to be reaching more than 150,000 children, teens and adults each year. And every step we take, we move forward "in the dark, trusting God!"

These historic words loom large in our minds and hearts. I can't tell you how many times we—as the leaders of Mount Hermon today—have revisited these words written by Hugh Gilchrest over a century ago. They have galvanized our desire to ensure we begin processing our decisions with prayer, since we want His will to be done at Mount Hermon "as it is in Heaven." Further, these words provide the needed steel in our resolve to trust fully in the Lord, to move forward "in the dark, trusting God," when we have no idea—humanly speaking—how He is going to provide. And then as we trust, we stand on tiptoes watching for Him to work!

That day in May 1906, and the pattern of prayer and trust, drove a stake in the ground beginning the establishment of a prayer/trust culture that exists to this day. Over and over, God has powerfully moved as we have followed this model. You'll witness that in the chapters to come. It drives us to our knees, it compels us to trust since we are continually moving forward "in the dark, trusting God!"

The earthquake and ensuing financial crisis were just the first of many difficulties the early leaders of Mount Hermon would endure as they laid the foundation of the ministry. In retrospect, those trials were exactly what they needed to keep *them* on their knees, trusting God. Read on.

THREE

TRIAL BY FIRE... & OTHER THINGS

In all this you greatly rejoice, though now for a little while you may have had to suffer grief in all kinds of trials. These have come so that the proven genuineness of your faith—of greater worth than gold, which perishes even though refined by fire—may result in praise, glory and honor when Jesus Christ is revealed.

1 PETER 1:6-7 (NIV)

G OD WAS IN THIS BEFORE THE EARTHQUAKE, AND HE WILL BE IN IT AFTER THE EARTHQUAKE. We will go on in the dark, trusting God.

The April 18, 1905 earthquake boldly demonstrated that the best of business models are still subject to the sovereignty of God. But the earthquake—and its ripple effects—were not the only challenge the leaders of Mount Hermon faced as they worked diligently to launch this new ministry—the first Christian camp and conference center in the United States west of the Mississippi River. Other significant hurdles—along with God's wonderful provision and blessings—were part of those early days. Back to the story...

After prayer, significant consultation and negotiation with the Arcadia Development Company following the earthquake, a new arrangement—with payment extending over a number of years—was agreed upon for the purchase of the property. The Board of Directors enthusiastically announced conferences would begin the summer of 1906, even though there were many unfinished details. The first public gathering, a Sunday service, occurred on June 24, 1906, for local residents and friends, some coming from as far away as Santa Cruz.

PREVIOUS Victory Circle 1923

As the first summer conferences progressed, interest and excitement increased, leading up to the climactic event to be held Sunday, July 22. Officially advertised as "Dedication Day," it immediately became known as "The Great Day" because of the tremendous exposure it brought to Mount Hermon.

Much of the anticipation focused on the special speaker for that service, fifty-year old R.A. Torrey, who had a list of accomplishments clearly setting him apart from other speakers of the day. Dwight L. Moody, for example, hired Torrey at age thirty-three, to run what would become known as Moody Bible Institute in Chicago. Not long after that appointment, he became pastor of what would eventually be called Moody Memorial Church. Over a four-year period, Torrey began an evangelistic tour giving him the opportunity to minister in nearly every English speaking country in the world, concluding in Great Britain near the end of 1905. Once home, Dr. Torrey accepted an invitation to speak at Mount Hermon for a week during our inaugural

Dr. R. A. Torrey

summer of 1906. (As an interesting aside, later in his life, Dr. Torrey played a significant role in the beginning of what would become known as Biola University and also served as pastor of the historic Church of the Open Door in downtown Los Angeles).

The meeting on "The Great Day" was scheduled to begin promptly at two o'clock in the afternoon. It was a typically warm mid-summer Sunday with just a hint of a cool ocean breeze. How many people would show up? It was anybody's guess. The leaders had prayed faithfully for a large turnout—and that's exactly what they got! Over a thousand people arrived by train and buggy, and some walked—all the way from San Jose. Depending on which account of that day you read, the numbers vary from twelve hundred to fifteen hundred.

A robust man with a full white beard, deep-set eyes, and an unflappable style, Dr. Torrey spoke powerfully from the top of a wooden platform, which had been erected "on the stream side of the road with his back to present Redwood Camp." In what would become a distinctive of Mount Hermon through the years—God showed up in powerful, life-changing ways. That day many accepted the clear invitation to receive Jesus Christ as personal Savior. What a way for the ministry of Mount Hermon to hit the ground running with an eternal impact.

Wouldn't it have been fun to be a conferee at Mount Hermon during that first summer? Thanks to the records of Rev. Henry Sanborne's daughter, Ruth, we catch a bit of the flavor of that era:

> *What a wonderful summer that was! Our family*
> *had previously spent a delightful vacation at Winona*
> *Lake (Indiana). And now to think that here on the Pacific*
> *Coast and so near home we had another Bible Conference*
> *grounds established! Our family occupied one of the cottage*
> *hotel rooms that surrounded Zayante Inn, and one of the*
> *guest tents. The dining room was part of the Inn. The*
> *meetings that summer were held in the hotel lounge or*
> *in the recreation room, which adjoined the bowling alley*
> *down by the creek. Through the rest of the year we lived in*
> *anticipation of the enjoyment which would be ours at the*
> *summer conference because my father had chosen his lot*
> *and we were to be in our own cottage the second summer.[1]*

Those early years were crucial to the spiritual foundation of the ministry. Gratefully, the men on the Board of Directors were committed to prayer, faithful in asking for the Lord's direction in their leadership. After seven summers, they felt it was time to evaluate the programs they had been offering. In the original history book on Mount Hermon, *Apart With Him*, Harry R. Smith summarizes the evaluation with these words:

> *After much prayer and thought they decided to simplify the conference program by reducing the number and variety of subjects treated and 'concentrating very largely upon special lines of Christian activity.' In a circular commenting upon the change in program, the administration stated 'Mount Hermon has a distinctive Christian mission in California. Its first great business is the teaching of the Bible and the promotion of missionary enterprise. The summer days are few at most—only some men and women with positive messages on main lines of service can be heard, and then only when they contribute directly on the main issues of the year. Persons who doubt the Bible or question the Master's missionary commission have no place on the Mount Hermon platform.* **It is not a rostrum of doubt** *(emphasis added).*[2]

This was a defining moment in Mount Hermon's history. Drawing a line in the sand, the Board chose not to deviate from the truth of the Word of God. The men chose to keep a "high view" of the Scriptures and treat them as authoritative and fully reliable. If you know anything about the history of the American church at that time, you will remember "Modernists" were confusing believers by questioning the authenticity of the Bible. Neo-orthodoxy and liberalism were making inroads in churches across many denominations. This decision by the Board charted the course we are still following today. In fact, the first item in Mount Hermon's Statement of Beliefs reads:

> *We believe in the verbal and complete inspiration by*
> *God of the original writings of the Old and New Testament*
> *Scriptures, the only infallible rule of faith and practice.*

When it comes to God's Word, Mount Hermon is definitely "not a rostrum of doubt!"

Then during the first week of April 1917, President Woodrow Wilson announced the United States was declaring war on Germany. A great number of people were pulled away from their businesses, schools and ministries, to assist in defending our country. Mount Hermon was not exempt from being affected. Family members of our staff and friends of Mount Hermon gave their lives for the freedom we enjoy today. Sugar rations became part of how people paid to come to conferences.

There are still good memories that surface as I think about this difficult time in our nation's history. One seemingly minor thing comes to mind that would cause major ripples in camps throughout the nation.

Campfires have always been a key element in the programming of camps and conference centers. Often they are places where we share what God has done in our hearts and what commitments we have made, or are making. In the early days, Mount Hermon's campfire was beautifully positioned in a clearing surrounded by Redwood trees, which create a natural amphitheater. From the beginning it had been referred to as "Vesper Circle."

But in 1917, in view of what God was doing in the lives of people attending Mount Hermon, and especially His saving work in the life of one lost young man, the conferees suggested the campfire

The first Victory Circle at Mount Hermon

be renamed "Victory Circle." As far as we know that was the first time a campfire was given that title. Today, however, you can find many camps and conference centers throughout the United States with the name "Victory Circle" on their property map.

In an amazing reoccurrence, April 18TH would once again be a day of trial and testing for Mount Hermon. The San Francisco earthquake struck April 18, 1905. April 18, 1921 would be remembered for another disaster—fire.

You may recall from the previous chapter, Tuxedo Property held a two-story hotel building called Hotel Tuxedo. When Mount Hermon purchased the property, leaders changed its name to Zayante Inn, since it was located close to Zayante Creek. As Harry Smith recorded with simplicity in *Apart With Him*:

Late on the night of April 18, 1921 a fire mysteriously
broke out in the Zayante Inn, burning it to the ground
together with all of its furnishings and the early Mount
Hermon records. It took with it most of the cottages which
surrounded the Inn, and what had been considered the
largest Madrone tree in Santa Cruz County. On top of that,
the Rev. James R. Platt, Mount Hermon's new General
Manager, was called home to be with the Lord.[3]

Zayante Inn was the central hub of activity for Mount Hermon
in those days, so imagine the significance of this disaster in relation
to the upcoming conferences, not to mention the loss of furnishings
and valuable records. Summer conferences were scheduled to begin
within several months. How could they possibly go forward in light
of this tragedy? Again, Harry Smith provides an excellent account
of God's answer to prayer:

This would be enough to dishearten even the most
courageous board of directors, but God has a way of
foreseeing such difficulties, and of arranging before hand
to place in positions of leadership men of his choosing who
either have the capabilities, or who rise to the occasion
and provide the leadership needed in times of real crisis.
Mount Hermon was to see the hand of God in that fashion,
in having placed in the presidency Mr. Albert Munger, a
business man of Berkeley...It was he upon whose shoulders
rested most heavily the problem of rebuilding Mount
Hermon from the ashes of the fire. It is a blessing that he
and the other officers and directors were men who trusted,
not in their own business knowledge and ingenuity, as
considerable as that was, but they trusted Him Who is
almighty, and Who overrules all and Who had told us that

'all things work together for good to them who love God, to them who are called according to His purpose.' [4]

News of the fire spread rapidly and prayer began in earnest. In the aftermath of the tragedy, friends of Mount Hermon stepped up to help. Others in the area made their cabins and homes available in order to house people during conferences that summer. Local groups provided food. Most significantly, God used the destruction of the inn's dining room as an incentive to expand the cafeteria in order to offer meals for full conferences. Once again, God's people prayed and He provided, redeeming the situation.

"God answers the prayers of His people, and His timing is always impeccable."

As only God can accomplish, the summer conferences of 1921 went off without a hitch. It's interesting to note, that summer one of the speakers was Dr. Sherman, the same man who inspired the early committee at Glenwood to go forward with the dream of building Mount Hermon. Also on the schedule was Dr. Harry Ironside, whose preaching and written commentaries discipled thousands of people in their study of the Word in the last half of the twentieth century.

Then in July of 1929, a full-scale forest fire burned out of control and moved quickly toward Mount Hermon. It was July and the grounds were full of conferees. While the property was valuable, human lives were at stake. Rapidly the situation became serious.

Ash fell on the rooftops of Mount Hermon's buildings. Staff were trying to arrange a train to quickly move the conferees out of harm's way, but with little success. With the fire bearing down, people did the one thing they could do to defend themselves.

They gathered in the auditorium and prayed—that God would intervene and save Mount Hermon with its marvelous groves of redwood trees. That He would save its summer homes and conference buildings. That no one would be injured. When the prayer meeting concluded, God's response was immediate and profound. Only He could have done such a thing.

The wind changed direction...a full 180 degrees! Now the fire burned away from Mount Hermon and everything was spared. Not long after the wind changed directions, some people decided to see just how close the fire had come to campus. They were amazed to find it had burned within a *few feet* of Mount Hermon's boundary line. But we never lost a tree, nor any buildings, and no one was hurt.

Much could be said about those early years of Mount Hermon. But two things stand out clearly...

...God answers the prayers of His people.

...And His timing is always impeccable.

FOUR

Igniting Eternal Sparks

May your deeds be shown to your servants,
your splendor to their children.

May the favor of the Lord our God rest on
us; establish the work of our hands for us—
yes, establish the work of our hands.

PSALMS 90:16–17 (NIV)

FROM ITS VERY FIRST CONFERENCE IN 1906, MOUNT HERMON HAS BEEN IN THE BUSINESS OF *REACHING PEOPLE FOR JESUS CHRIST.* We want to create places and experiences where people can encounter Jesus in such a way that their lives are transformed! No matter what has gone on in a person's life prior to coming here, we take people just as they are. Mount Hermon has been a place of many significant spiritual decisions—of igniting eternal fires.

Initially, Mount Hermon was a place for adults and families, but in the 20s and 30s our outreach expanded to young people, hitting its stride in the decade of the 30s. Much of that had to do with a remarkable woman.

Miss Henrietta Mears was nothing short of a human dynamo, spiritually speaking. She propelled hundreds of young people into a life-changing relationship with the Lord, many going on to vocational Christian service. The numbers of young adults she reached are staggering.

Born in 1889 in Fargo, North Dakota, Henrietta attended the University of Minnesota, graduating with a degree in science. For nearly fifteen years she taught high school in Minnesota. Then in

PREVIOUS Young singer 1940s

1928, after a trip to the West Coast the previous year, she felt drawn to move to California. With a round face, piercing eyes behind an ever-present pair of eyeglasses, and a penchant for stylish hats, Henrietta Mears who remained single all of her life, was one of a kind. All who knew her agree her most productive ministry occurred when she made the move to Hollywood to become the Director of Christian Education at Hollywood Presbyterian Church.

The stories of how God used her ministry are incredible. It didn't take long before her Sunday School programs attracted four thousand children and young people. She particularly loved working with teens and college-aged young adults, and her weekly Bible studies drew close to five hundred individuals.

Henrietta Mears, front row, fifth from the left at a Mount Hermon Young People's Conference in 1930

Mount Hermon had launched its Young People's Conferences and Henrietta somehow heard what was happening here and decided to do some research on her own. Her personal assistant, Ethel May Baldwin, shared about the decision to send students to us:

She heard of Mount Hermon and the new Young
People's Conference and sent four persons from the college
department to 'spy out the land.' They came back with such
glowing reports that in 1931 we sent up 80, and after that
200 each summer through 1937.[1]

Miss Mears was thrilled with what happened in those Young People's Conferences at Mount Hermon. Many from her groups at Hollywood Presbyterian accepted the Lord, and many, as a result, chose to follow the Lord's call into ministry. One young man's life was totally redirected.

———— • • • ————

Richard was born in North Dakota in 1916. A handsome young man, he attended Valley City State Teacher's College in Valley City, but North Dakota was too small for his dreams. He longed to be a professional jazz "scat" singer and a famous actor. There was only one place to go in order to be discovered. Richard moved to Hollywood.

Walking along the streets of that "movie-land" one cold night in January 1936, he heard the glorious sound of music coming from the "annex" of Hollywood Presbyterian Church. Curious, he stumbled into a college meeting with none other than Miss Mears at the head of the room!

Richard became fascinated with Henrietta's teaching of the Word of God and began attending her weekly meetings. By March of that year he had accepted the Lord Jesus as His personal Savior and a few months later, he was on his way to the Young People's Conference at Mount Hermon. Richard describes this experience in his own words:

I remember with deep gratitude the little fellowship
groups, which would meet after the big meetings (at Mount

*Hermon) when we would get on our knees and pour out our
hearts together to the Lord seeking an awakening upon
the whole Church and getting a vision for the whole world.
Those memories are etched unforgettably in my mind.
When I came to Mount Hermon first, I was a young fellow,
four years out of high school. I had been in college two years
and then out working. From the age of ten I had aspired
to a career on stage or screen. Most of my life had been
spent furthering such a career. The opportunity to come to
Hollywood came in 1935, and I jumped at it. After a year of
discouragement I was offered a seven-year contract. Then,
a few days at Mount Hermon transformed my life and
changed every plan.*

*Although I received Christ as my Savior sitting in an
automobile with Dave Cowie on a Sunday afternoon in
March, 1936, my first really deep experience with Christ
came that summer in July during the Young People's
Conference. That was my first Bible Conference and, as
a new Christian, I looked forward to it with tremendous
anticipation. So much so, in fact, that during the first
three days of the conference I was greatly disillusioned; in
addition to which, of course, under the disillusionment, I
began to question whether or not I really wanted to go
on in the Christian faith. The thing came to a head on
Wednesday afternoon when I asked my pastor, Dave Cowie,
to let me go home. Very wisely, he told me that he would
allow me to go home the next day if I would attend the
Wednesday evening meetings with an open heart,
which I did.*

*The speaker that evening was Dr. George McCune,
veteran missionary (Korea) who had suffered much for his
faith and his work for Christ. It was as if Dr. McCune was*

speaking directly to me, 'I want you to go to Korea as a
missionary.' I simply rejected it and left the meeting greatly
disturbed.

As I came out of the auditorium, Miss Mears noticed
me and urged me to attend a prayer meeting at her cottage,
which I did. It was while we were on our knees in the
dark in that cottage that I gave myself to Jesus Christ for
whatever He would lead me to do and I enjoyed the greatest,
deepest peace I'd ever known in my life up to that time.

Because of that experience, I determined to go to
Wheaton College in the fall, get my degree and go on to
Princeton Theological Seminary, planning then to be a
candidate for missions in Korea.[2]

Richard did eventually complete his schooling at Wheaton
and Princeton, but he never made it to Korea. God unmistakably
moved him to become a pastor.

When Rachel and I first connected with Richard, it was during
our years in Washington D.C. (which I'll get to later when I share
a bit of our story). "Dick" was Senior Minister of the amazing
congregation at Fourth Presbyterian Church in Bethesda, Maryland.
It was a position he held from 1958 until 1981 when he left to pastor
an even more amazing congregation—he became the Chaplain of
the United States Senate.

This young man, who in 1936 at Mount Hermon gave his life
to minister for Jesus Christ wherever that might be, was the man
who would one day hold one of the most significant Christian
leadership positions in our nation. It was the perfect profession
for him. Dick loved to disciple men—it was a special passion of
his—and during our years in Washington, he became one of the
most significant mentors I would have in my life. I fondly recall his

admonitions for Christians to be "God's agents of His truth, grace, and love" wherever God placed us.

Obviously, I'm talking about Dr. Richard C. Halverson.

Years later, in 1999, I had the privilege of attending the National Prayer Breakfast, a function that was one of Dick's passions. At the conclusion of the day, many of us met together for something called the Fellowship Dinner. After the meal, I waited to talk with Dick and he asked me what I was doing.

"I'm the Executive Director at a camp out in California called Mount Hermon," I replied, having no idea of his history here.

He grasped my arms. "I love Mount Hermon! Do you know about me and Mount Hermon?"

"You know about us?" I responded, incredulous, since I had only known Dr. Halverson as a high-profile pastor on the East cCoast.

That's when he shared the story you have just read. As he always did, he encouraged me in my leadership

Dr. Richard Halverson

here. And I will never forget his final words to me as we parted, the last time I saw him on earth. Looking at me with eyes glowing with intensity, he said, "Mount Hermon is so important, Roger. Handle it well!"

◆———— • • • ————◆

Richard was just one of the young adults Mount Hermon and Miss Mears impacted. Robert was another one who God used in huge ways.

Robert was a local boy, growing up in the San Francisco Bay area. In fact, his family had a cottage on the grounds of Mount Hermon—18 Parkway—up by what is now Ponderosa Lodge. Robert spent a good deal of time at Mount Hermon. He reflects:

> *At a Christian Endeavor Conference while I was in*
> *junior high school, I believe that I knew a touch of the*
> *Spirit in a Victory Circle meeting. But my interest in Mount*
> *Hermon and the things of the Lord lagged.* [3]

You've heard stories like this—a good kid exposed to the things of the Lord, but less than excited about allowing the Lord to direct his life. What would be the catalyst God would use to get Robert on track spiritually?

During one of the weeks in 1931, Henrietta Mears brought up her group from Hollywood and Bob was here from the University of Berkeley at his parent's' request:

> *It was not until my junior year in college that I*
> *returned at the urging of my parents—but on the condition*
> *that they not expect me to go to meetings! I only wanted*
> *a vacation. Through the influence of an attractive girl*
> *from Hollywood who I met in the Fountain, I found myself*
> *attending Victory Circle and other meetings. The young*
> *people from Hollywood impressed me greatly as night after*
> *night they gave witness to what the Lord was doing in*
> *their lives. Finally on the last night of the conference at the*
> *(campfire) service, I made my commitment to Christ.* [4]

For the second time the campfire service at Victory Circle became a significant part of Bob's movement toward God's will for his life.

> *I admit that there was such pressure that my hands*
> *were cold. On that night Dr. Sutherland was in charge,*
> *which made it more difficult for me because he knew me*
> *well. We didn't fill Victory Circle, so there was a margin*
> *there of use. When a person made a decision he went*

down to the front, put a (stick) on the fire, and then sat in another place. This was like separating the sheep from the goats! The longer the meeting went on the lonelier one got because all those around were leaving. I sweated that out for two hours before I made a decision. That was very real pressure! But it was the pressure of the Holy Spirit and I am glad that I was under that kind of pressure. I couldn't escape it. I was confronted with the question: What was I going to do with Christ? There it was! I had to make a decision one way or the other. I knew it would make demands on me and change the direction of my life, especially when I returned to the University of California and my fraternity. But the Lord entered my life that night and from that time on I had a personal relationship to Jesus Christ.[5]

Robert finished UC Berkeley and then went on to Moody Bible Institute, and Princeton Seminary, eventually becoming Senior Pastor at First Presbyterian Church of Berkeley, California for over twenty-five years. Have you figured out who Robert was?

Dr. Robert Boyd Munger. If his name sounds familiar to you, it could be you've heard of or read his best-selling booklet entitled *My Heart, Christ's Home*, a book about completely surrendering to the Lord Jesus.

Bob also served as a professor at Fuller Theological Seminary in Pasadena, California for many years. But he always kept his little cottage up the road on 18 Parkway.

In 2001, shortly before he went to be with Jesus, I visited Bob at his Mount Hermon home. At ninety years of age, he confessed that more than anything, he was ready to go home to Heaven. He spoke earnestly. "Roger, I keep asking the Lord, 'Why do You keep me here?'"

"Has He answered your question?" I asked.

"Yes. But do you know what He told me?"

"What?"

Robert Boyd Munger and wife, Edith

He paused. "The Lord told me to be *thankful.* He told me to be *grateful.* He told me to share the reasons for my gratitude with every person I meet."

"That's wonderful," I replied. "You have heard from Heaven."

"And that includes you," Bob interjected. With that, frail, ninety-year-old Bob Munger shared blessing upon blessing that the Lord had showered on him over his lifetime.

As I left his home that afternoon to walk down the hill to my office, I wept. How many of us as we age become critical and even bitter? He couldn't stop talking about all the richness in his life because of Jesus! He has spent hours expressing his gratitude for things large and small. As I walked down that hill I asked God to help me follow Bob's example. Coming from a brittle diabetic man, who had experienced a series of strokes and could no longer effectively care for himself, Bob just wanted to thank and praise! It was a powerful life lesson…one I have never forgotten.

Spiritually speaking, it was ignited at a campfire.

———— • • • ————

The following is the story of another man who was influenced here at Mount Hermon: His name was Cliff and he came to Mount Hermon from his home in Ceres, California, a small town just south of Modesto. At age ten or eleven Cliff attended Redwood, our children's camp. Like Victory Circle, Redwood Camp had its own campfire back then called Redwood Circle or the Redwood Bowl.

And just like Victory Circle, Redwood Circle was a place where God touched hearts.

Back in 2002, I wrote Cliff a letter and asked him to reflect on what happened that night sitting around the campfire in 1934. Here is part of his reply:

Dear Roger:

I have many happy memories of Mount Hermon. It has figured so very positively in my spiritual journey from my earliest youth. I dedicated my life to Christ at a campfire service in Redwood Circle under the ministry of Dick Hillis around 1934...
...I rejoice in God's continued hand of blessing upon its ministry.
Thank you and God bless you.

> *Sincerely,*
> *Cliff*

For all of us who have been impacted by the global ministry of Billy Graham, this little boy who dedicated his life to Christ at Redwood Circle grew up to become the Director of Music for the Billy Graham Evangelistic team, as well as the Program Director for The Hour of Decision radio broadcast.

Little Cliff was Cliff Barrows.

———— • • • ————

For every Dick Halverson, Bob Munger, and Cliff Barrows, there are scores of folks just like you and me who love God and want Him to use us in our everyday lives. Our Heavenly Father loves and cherishes anyone who makes the choice to accept Jesus' gift of salvation. He is no respecter of persons. Whether you make a decision for Christ at Mount Hermon or somewhere else, God loves you passionately. Whether you end up in vocational ministry at an international level, teach a class of third graders in a public school, help folks as a cashier in a grocery store, work as a lawyer, doctor or professor, you are equally valued by the Lord. God scatters His children as agents of his love and grace throughout all the strata of our society. I simply tell the stories of these three men so you can catch a flicker of some of the eternal sparks that have been ignited at Mount Hermon ...

...around campfires.

FIVE

Unplanned Global Impact

But you will receive power when the Holy Spirit comes on you; and you will be my witnesses in Jerusalem, and in all Judea and Samaria, and to the ends of the earth.

ACTS 1:8 (NIV)

WE CAN'T FOCUS ON THE STORY OF GOD'S WORK AT MOUNT HERMON IN ISOLATION. Its history was certainly influenced by the events impacting our nation. In 1939, WWII began with Germany's blitzkrieg attack of Poland. After Pearl Harbor in 1941, the United States entered the war and committed the full resources of this nation to defeating the Axis powers. During this time, many things were altered in the way Americans lived their daily lives. For a nation that spent most of its time focused on domestic affairs, Americans then turned their attention to events beyond our shores.

As the war raged on in Europe and the Pacific, young people who would normally have attended our conferences were across the ocean fighting for our freedom. Add to that the rationing of gasoline and tires for those on home shores, and it was becoming increasingly difficult for people to visit Mount Hermon.

And don't forget Mount Hermon's location. When Pearl Harbor was attacked by the Japanese on Sunday morning, December 7, 1941, the entire West Coast was put on alert for the possibility of attack. Everyone living here dealt with an atmosphere of fear hanging like a cloud over life in general.

PREVIOUS JEMS 60TH Anniversary (partial) Group Photo

Harry Smith recounts two specific Mount Hermon-related incidents in his book, *Apart With Him*, that illustrate this fact:

> *All aspects of American life were immediately altered,*
> *and Mount Hermon was no exception. The Pacific Coast*
> *was immediately alerted against the possibility of Japanese*
> *attack by land, sea, or air. One unforgettable impression*
> *of those early war days was that of a meeting of the Board*
> *of Directors held on the night of December 12, 1941 in one*
> *of the private dining rooms of the Y W C A in San Francisco.*
> *Shortly after President George Campbell of San Jose called*
> *the meeting to order, there was a general air raid warning*
> *with the result that every electric light in San Francisco*
> *was extinguished. The meeting stopped for a while,*
> *anticipating that the lights would go on again, but when it*
> *became apparent that they might not do so for some time,*
> *the meeting was continued in absolute darkness. It was not*
> *until the meeting was almost finished that the 'all clear'*
> *signal was given and the lights could be turned on again.*
> *The secretary scanned eagerly the notes which he had taken*
> *in the complete darkness and fortunately found that he was*
> *able to decipher them.*[1]
>
> *One of the problems which confronted the Board at*
> *this time was the fact that a number of the speakers who*
> *had been lined up for the summer season of 1942 sent*
> *messages indicating that they thought they should give up*
> *any thought of traveling to the West Coast.*[2]

Yet those problems seemed minuscule when compared to the loss of life. World War II touched many families with the deaths of sons, fathers and other family members. Hundreds who had come regularly to Mount Hermon gave their lives in battle or died as a result of mistreatment in Prisoner of War camps. In their honor, Mount Hermon established a fund to erect a building auspiciously named the Youth Memorial Building. Those who gave $100 or more toward the fund were free to have the name of a departed family member engraved on a special brass plaque, displayed permanently in the building. You can still go into Youth Memorial and read the names of some of those young men who gave their lives for our freedom.

As the war continued, anger began bubbling to the surface against Japanese people in America, especially in light of the surprise attack on Pearl Harbor. They were marked as "the enemy." Many Americans were suspicious of them, assuming they were spies quietly working on elaborate espionage plans to take over our country. History proved this mindset wrong, but at the time it seemed plausible.

It is a terrible blot on our country's past that as many as 120,000 Japanese-Americans were forced to leave their homes in California and live in Internment Camps in remote areas, no matter what their sentiment was regarding the war. One internee, Raymond Ono, was eleven years old when his family was taken from his home in California. At eighty years of age and a retired judge, he recalled the experience vividly in an article in the *Wall Street Journal*:

> *Mr. Ono recalls giving away his prized red bike in the days before his family was interred. He remembers the day his father collapsed with heart failure in the barracks— and that, by the time the camp doctor had arrived, his father's body was cold.*
>
> *Just as painful for Mr. Ono were the years after the war. Each survivor got $25 and a train ticket. Most had no homes to return to, no job waiting; they faced such discrimination, some had trouble even finding a grocery store that would take their money.*[3]

No less than three U.S. Presidents (Gerald Ford, Ronald Reagan, George H.W. Bush) have publicly apologized for the unjust treatment of Japanese-Americans in those days, but it doesn't take away the pain and agony of what they lived through during that awful period. It would take years to rebuild their lives and families.

The Board members of Mount Hermon began asking what could be done to heal rather than add to the pain of their disastrous situation. One thing was clear—Japanese people would be welcome at our conferences. Harry Smith described this period at Mount Hermon. He wrote the following in his book in 1951, when anti-Japanese sentiment was still emotionally potent:

> *Nevertheless, sentiment against the Japanese ran quite strong and it was some time after the war was over before many Japanese felt free to return to their former homes in California. In 1947 a few Japanese Christians attended some of the young people's conferences at Mount Hermon. In 1948 there was even a larger number, still larger in 1949 and by 1950 a separate conference for Japanese young people was arranged at Redwood Camp June 19TH to 25TH.*
>
> *(The June 1950 conference) was attended by one hundred fifty Japanese young people including many non-Christians. By the time the week was over, thirty of them had made a public profession of Christ as their Savior.*[4]

The Lord was at work! Just a month before, in May of 1950, a group of American-born Japanese ministers gathered at Mount Hermon for a prayer retreat. They came away from that experience convinced they should form a society "to encourage, challenge and awaken interest in revival, evangelism and missions." That was the birth of the Japanese Evangelical Missionary Society—JEMS as we know it.

Written in a piece of their early literature, JEMS defined itself as follows:

> It is a voluntary fellowship of evangelical Christian pastors and laymen to promote revival, evangelism, and missions in local churches. For many years faithful Christians had been praying for a spiritual awakening among the Japanese churches of America. This burden developed into prayer fellowships among a score of Nisei (American-born Japanese) ministers in northern and southern California.
>
> In May 1950, at Mount Hermon during a joint prayer retreat, the attendant ministers felt impelled to form a society in order to encourage, challenge, and awaken interest in revival, evangelism, and missions. After a definite confirmation of the Holy Spirit the newly formed society was named the Japanese Evangelical Missionary Society and legally incorporated in June, 1951.[5]

Every summer since that time, the JEMS group has met for a week of family conference at Mount Hermon. They are part of the very fabric of our summer schedule and we always look forward to having them with us. For me, this is one of the high points of Mount Hermon's history—at a time when many Americans were isolating and discriminating against these American citizens, Mount Hermon reached out and welcomed them as brothers and sisters in the Lord and part of God's family. We feel a special "kinship" with JEMS and are honored to host their major conference each year. Further, they are a constant reminder of how God is using guests that attend our conferences to create a truly *global impact*.

We now have great relationships with organizations such as World Vision, REACH Global, and Compassion International, to name a few. Members and leaders come to Mount Hermon to discuss important aspects of their ministries, to pray about specific challenges facing them, to hear God speak from His Word, to plan for the future, and to get spiritually re-charged. It's not a stretch to say the ministry of Mount Hermon goes with them to the four corners of the world.

Here are some specific areas of outreach we know about, from just those three groups that meet here at Mount Hermon:

WORLD VISION

Mexico
Dominican Republic
Columbia
Peru
Brazil
Bolivia
Chile
Angola
Mozambique
Zambia
Zimbabwe
South Africa
Finland
Russia Federation
Singapore
Indonesia
Australia
New Zealand

COMPASSION INTERNATIONAL

- Canada
- United Kingdom
- Netherlands
- Spain
- Germany
- Australia
- New Zealand

REACH GLOBAL

- Cyprus
- Morocco
- Algeria
- Togo
- Liberia
- Middle East
- Iran

Director Ed Hayes with the JEMS leadership 1980s

North Asia
Asia
South Asia
Southeast Asia
Philippines

Recently, Murphy Felton—one of our staff members—was doing research for an article that was to be included in an upcoming issue of the Mount Hermon LOG and found that "a missionary embedded deep in the Underground Church in Tehran came (to Mount Hermon) for a few days and left rejuvenated and energized to go back and continue ministering to those in an oppressed land." Her excitement was palpable.

> *"Mission agencies gather to seek God's wisdom on where each of their missionaries should be stationed. Financial directors of world-wide mission organizations use their 'time away' to pray how best to distribute the financial resources the Lord provides."* [6]

Just as Murphy exudes joy in how God is using Mount Hermon across the globe, I, too, am thrilled to see God at work around the world through this ministry.

We recently had three hundred and forty Iranian Christians gathered together in our auditorium singing praises to God in the Farsi language. I am eternally grateful Mount Hermon had the courage from the very beginning of its existence to minister to everyone as I believe Jesus would do were He on earth. And the Lord has certainly honored that commitment.

One ethnic group that has become a particular favorite of mine is our Latino community. The demographic data I read shows the Latino population as the fastest growing ethnic group in the state of California (as well as the whole United States), so it's important for us to be a place where Latinos feel welcome and ministered to.

Their family bonds are truly admirable. How they love to sing, to give testimony, to pray, and they love the teaching of God's Word. You need only wander by their meeting rooms to understand immediately how enthralled they are with things of the Lord. They bring joy and enthusiasm to all they do! Everything seems to be an act of worship and celebration.

I could go on and on with stories of how the ministry of Mount Hermon is truly having a global impact, but I think you get the point. What initially started with our JEMS conference during those years of prejudice following WWII, is expanding to touch every major continent. It's a topic that gets our entire staff excited. We love to see God at work in the lives of people who go from our grounds to places all over the world.

And late in 2012, we entered into a strategic alliance with the folks from the first Christian conference center in mainland China—at their request—to consult with them on programming and recreation ideas. Further, we'll be sending summer missionaries to help lead their children's programming. Our vision for the future includes being involved in at least three of these strategic alliances, helping Christian camps and conference centers in other nations.

When asked about the privilege of working with some of these major mission organizations, Sharon Renwick, a staff member who works closely with them, replied, "Our staff truly understands and lives out the ministry of hospitality. We come alongside, sharing the same heart and purpose. As a staff we are praying for them even before they get here, and when they arrive we take time to pray with them. We're in this together, because we're all part of the Kingdom. We often hear back from the leaders that those times of prayer together were an especially meaningful part of the conference for them. We're here for ministry and they really get that."

Did you notice what Sharon highlighted as an important part of working together? Prayer! There it is again.

Hearing from Heaven is part of reaching the world at Mount Hermon.

SIX

A Special Guest With Prophetic Prayer

The prayer of a righteous person
is powerful and effective.

JAMES 5:16B (NIV)

W E'VE ALREADY TALKED ABOUT JULY 24, 1906
—"The Great Day"—when Dr. R. A. Torrey came to
Mount Hermon and spoke to somewhere between
twelve hundred and fifteen hundred people. By today's standards,
that's a lot of people on the grounds of Mount Hermon! And
remember, there were few automobiles in those days. Most of the
people arrived by train, others came by horse and wagon, and some
walked. In any case, it would be more than fifty years before Mount
Hermon saw attendance numbers like these again.

Almost fifty-two years later, on July 11, 1958, another
well-known person came to speak at Mount Hermon. In order to
accommodate the crowds that were expected, the fifteen hundred
seats necessary for the audience that heard Dr. Torrey would have
to be increased by one thousand. To twenty-five hundred!

Who could draw that many people? In 1999, he would appear
in Gallup's List of Most Widely Admired People in the Twentieth
Century, recorded seventh behind Mother Theresa, Martin Luther
King, Jr., John Kennedy, Albert Einstein, Helen Keller, and Franklin
Roosevelt. The Pope finished eighth, Eleanor Roosevelt and Winston

PREVIOUS Billy Graham, Jim and Bud Kennedy, Bill and Colette Gwinn touring Mount Hermon

Churchill rounded out the top ten. You've probably guessed it—Billy Graham! And Billy was coming to speak at Mount Hermon.

Mount Hermon's Board of Directors knew Billy was scheduled for a crusade in the Bay Area during the Spring of 1958, so in March of that year, they wrote inviting him and his team to speak for a week of meetings at the Conference Center. To their delight, Dr. Graham agreed as long as they would allow him to speak only one of the days, with two of his team handling the rest of the week. The Board agreed to that arrangement.

The Billy Graham Bay Area Crusade began Sunday, April 27, 1958, in the Cow Palace in San Francisco with phenomenal crowds in attendance. The San Francisco Chronicle quoted the manager of the Cow Palace as saying, "There were at least eighteen thousand people crowded inside and five thousand people standing in the parking lot...and more than two thousand automobiles had to be turned away."

Because of the enormous crowds, Billy spoke twice that evening to accommodate as many as possible. First he addressed the five thousand in the parking lot while the opening music and program were taking place inside the Cow Palace. Then he hustled inside, just in time to speak to the eighteen thousand waiting for him there.

That one evening offers a tiny glimpse of what it was like to be Billy Graham in 1958. Add to that the fact that his meetings at the Cow Palace continued for six weeks, and you can begin to understand the impact the Billy Graham Evangelistic Association had around the country and the world.

Under the capable direction of Mount Hermon's new Executive Director, Bill Gwinn, the staff began praying, planning and preparing with excitement for the week with Billy and his team. They quickly realized this event would be gigantic. One of the first things they needed to do was ask Dr. Graham to speak twice on July 11TH, instead of the one time he had agreed to. He was willing, so then plans began in earnest.

How was the staff to choose which twenty-five hundred people should be invited to each session? More to the point, how could they seat so many people? Feed such a crowd? Where could they park their cars? There were a myriad of details to think through for an event of this magnitude.

A ticket system was instituted. Conference registrants, property owners, staff and their guests received tickets for the afternoon session. Tickets for the evening session were carefully distributed among local business owners in Felton, Ben Lomond, Boulder Creek, Camp Evers and Santa Cruz, with instructions that they give them to people who would enjoy hearing Dr. Graham and appreciate being introduced to Mount Hermon.

The obvious choice of where to hold the meetings was the auditorium, but there would have to be additional seating–much

Director Bill Gwinn shakes hands with Dr Graham

more than was typically available. Not only was every existing chair used to surround the auditorium, portable bleachers were brought in from San Lorenzo Valley High School, which helped provide adequate seating outside for the expected crowd.

Plans were made to serve meals in the dining room, a huge challenge with so many people on the grounds. Various guests were rotated in and out as seats became available. The Board of Directors and their wives were privileged to share a special luncheon with Dr. Graham and his team. Today, a black and white photograph of that event hangs in the hallway just outside my office.

The parking issue was major. Thankfully, along with the regular parking spots at the Conference Center, local Mount Hermon residents offered to give up their personal spots. Once those spaces filled, overflow parking was available at the Evangelical Free Church on Graham Hill Road, as well as Felton Presbyterian Church. Buses on loan from Felton Presbyterian Church, Twin Lakes Church, and Calvary Baptist Church of Los Gatos shuttled folks from these overflow lots to the Conference Center.

After all the prayer, planning and preparation, our Spiritual Life Mission Week kicked off on July 6TH and ran through July 12TH. Two of Billy Graham's associates, Leighton Ford and Joe Blinco, taught throughout the first part of the week.

Finally the big day was here. Friday, July 11, 1958 dawned warm and sunny with temperatures in the eighties. Visitors outside scrambled to find even a bit of shade under one of the majestic redwoods. The afternoon crowd arrived and the first service began. On the back wall of the platform hung our traditional wooden plank with the annual theme or verse hand-painted on it. How appropriate that the theme for 1958 was "To God be the Glory."

Cliff Barrows—yes, the same Cliff Barrows who over twenty years before had given his life to Christ as an eleven-year-old boy at Redwood Camp—opened the service by leading the group in some familiar hymns. George Beverly Shea sang a solo, the auditorium resounding with his deep, rich bass voice. Tall, tan, and fashionably dressed in a gray-blue suit, Dr. Graham rose to speak from the Mount Hermon pulpit, reading his text from Matthew 18:3:

> *Verily I say unto you, Except ye be converted and become as little children, ye shall not enter into the kingdom of heaven.*

In his simple yet profound manner, he delivered a message inviting those who had never met Jesus to accept Him, but he also wisely included encouragement for many of the guests who had become recent believers through the Bay Area Crusade.

That evening, the second meeting occurred. And fulfilling the hope of the staff and Boards, the auditorium overflowed with visitors brand new to Mount Hermon. Twenty-four hundred people attended the Friday evening service and when asked how many had never been to Mount Hermon before, seventy percent of the crowd raised their hands high.

Once again Cliff Barrows led the crowd in singing and George Beverly Shea sang a solo before Billy rose to deliver his passionate message of Good News. Again he gave an invitation to receive Jesus as Savior and Lord, inviting those who did to make their decision public. Typically he would have invited people to come to the front for counseling, but because of the size of the crowd, that was impossible. Instead, he asked those who were receiving the Lord to lift their hand.

Hundreds of hands flew up that evening!

Counseling space had been set up in the dining room, where one of Billy's associate evangelists, Joe Blinco, provided follow-up for those who had made a decision to follow Jesus Christ as Savior. Included were thirty soldiers who had come with a group of one hundred from Fort Ord, a seventy-five-year-old gentleman, and a family of five. Some of those family members still attend Mount Hermon today.

Executive Director Bill Gwinn reflected:

> *Few events in Mount Hermon's history have held the excitement of Billy Graham's visit. Not only was it a special privilege to have this Christian statesman ministering on our grounds, but many in our surrounding community met Christ through his ministry. To see the dining room as the scene of counseling for hundreds of newborn Christians is a sight I shall never forget.*[1]

Amazingly, during all the busyness of that day, somehow Billy was able to sneak away in a Jeep for a tour of the grounds. Jim Kennedy and his son, Bud, made their Jeep available, so Bill and Colette Gwinn and Billy Graham climbed in.

Jim drove them from the Conference Center down to Redwood Camp, eventually ending up on Graham Hill Road, where they stopped to appreciate the beautiful panorama of the San Lorenzo Valley. They drove even higher, up to Pine Plateau, where the redwoods were replaced by Ponderosa pines. Dr. Graham was absolutely enthralled.

Billy Graham, Bill Gwinn, and others on tour, July 1958

"Boy, I love this hill!" he exclaimed. "It reminds me so much of our home in Montreat, North Carolina."

To reach the cross on the top of the hill they had to drive through property owned by Kaiser Industries—the Sand and Gravel Division. Bill Gwinn explained to Dr. Graham that Mount Hermon had approached Kaiser about the possibility of purchasing this land but had been turned down. He emphasized how crucial it was in the development of Mount Hermon's ministry—how much greater effectiveness we would have for the Lord if we owned it. It could, in time, become the site for a new youth camp specifically focused on reaching teens with the Gospel.

Dr. Graham listened carefully, obviously grasping Bill's urgency. Surprising everyone, he interrupted:

"Let's stop right now and claim this hill for the Lord!"

And that's exactly what they did. Billy Graham prayed a simple prayer of faith, thanking God that the Kaiser property would be given to Mount Hermon.

It shouldn't surprise any of us that his prayer was prophetic. What Billy Graham prayed for that day in 1958 became a reality eleven years later. On March 13, 1969, A. Ford Lovelace, Vice President of Kaiser Industries and General Manager of Kaiser Sand and Gravel presented Bill Gwinn with the deed to 10.58 acres of land. It was a gift to Mount Hermon! You know this property as Ponderosa Lodge.

> *"Let's stop right now and claim this hill for the Lord!"*

Ponderosa Lodge was built and officially dedicated fourteen months later with Mount Hermon Board President, John Jenks, leading the celebration. A young Ponderosa Lodge counselor, Don Broesamle (who came to know Jesus as his Savior at Redwood Camp), shared his excitement about Ponderosa being used to minister to teenagers. One of the highlights of the ceremony was reading a special telegram. Its author congratulated Mount Hermon on this great accomplishment and expressed gratitude that in those troubled times a fine facility would be available to the youth of the state for the study of the Bible and Christian principles. The telegram was signed by the Governor of California—Ronald Reagan.

Over and over in the history of Mount Hermon, people have prayed, heard from Heaven, trusted God in the dark, and God has clearly demonstrated He is always at work. In this instance the person starting that process was Billy Graham, but he has no corner on the market when it comes to talking to the Lord. Your prayers are just as important as his or anyone else's. Are you asking God for something big in your life right now? Take it from us, He's listening and He's already got it handled!

SEVEN

Prayer Moves ...Roads?

I am the LORD, the God of all mankind.
Is anything too hard for me?

JEREMIAH 32:27 (NIV)

I T WAS A BIT LONGER THAN A DECADE BETWEEN BILLY
GRAHAM'S VISIT TO MOUNT HERMON IN 1958, AND THE
ANSWER TO HIS PRAYER REGARDING THE GIFT OF LAND
IN 1969. During that same period of time, there was another event
at Mount Hermon that has to be described as nothing short of a
miracle!

Conference Drive, which runs through the middle of Mount
Hermon used to be the major roadway to get from Felton to Scotts
Valley and beyond. It had been this way since Mount Hermon was
founded. Normal traffic, including large gravel trucks, traveled it
every day. So did Mount Hermon's guests. They crossed that busy
road to get from their rooms to the Administration Building, to
the dining room, the Book Shop, auditorium and swimming pool.
There were no traffic signals, caution lights or crossing guards. It
was an extremely dangerous situation, and at its worst in the years
between 1958 and 1969.

Originally named Scotts Valley Road, during most of its
history it was known as Mount Hermon Road. As early as 1912,
letters and records show this narrow, dusty trail as the "primary
road system" for the area.

PREVIOUS Conference Drive 1950s

The "dusty trail" years continued until 1927, when the county of Santa Cruz decided to pave the road, despite significant protests from Mount Hermon's Board of Directors. Even then, our Board could envision the problems that would occur due to increased traffic. Since Mount Hermon Road was the major route between Scotts Valley and the whole San Lorenzo Valley, traffic was growing almost daily. Against all the issues related to pedestrian safety, the county went ahead with the paving. One of the Board members made the following assessment at the August, 1931 meeting:

> *The reconstruction of the county road has been*
> *of much concern and anxiety. Now that it is completed,*
> *automobiles go through at a high speed and lives are*
> *constantly endangered.*[1]

This concern in 1931 escalated into a dangerous situation by the late 1950s. Mount Hermon Director Bill Gwinn expressed publicly that it was only a matter of time before a fatal accident occurred. In an interview, Bill later reflected:

> *Every day hundreds of campers looked both ways (most*
> *of the time) before they crossed the road from their lodging*
> *center to the dining center and meeting rooms. It was a*
> *miracle that despite the heavy traffic, there were no deaths.*[2]

Bill reasoned his case over and over with county officials—to no avail. He finally traveled to the state capitol in Sacramento to plead his case, but no one seemed to care. In 1959, the Board sought an injunction against the sand and log companies that were hauling their loads through campus on enormous trucks—at an average rate of forty trucks per hour each day! By the end of the 1950s, it was estimated that twelve hundred cars, trucks, and trailers were using the road daily.

In 1965, a much-needed pedestrian overpass was constructed between the Administration Building and the Chapel, thanks to a gracious gift provided by long time Mount Hermon constituents, the Chamberlain family. As a result, pedestrians could cross the busy road by walking above the traffic. It was helpful, but still there were children and adults dodging traffic in areas not convenient to the overpass.

By 1968, traffic had swelled to 16,000 vehicles *per day*. From the findings in another report at the time, the two-lane Mount Hermon Road took second place in traffic use only to the California state freeways in the region (along with Highway 17) There seemed no reasonable solution in sight to this hazardous situation.

> *"Bill then saw that if Mount Hermon Road could be closed due to some major 'natural phenomenon,' there may be a possible solution to the dilemma they faced."*

The best idea was to build a bypass road that could handle all the traffic without putting anyone in danger. The idea became known as "the Mount Hermon Bypass." Unfortunately, there was no financial support from the only source of help, the State. And it seemed unlikely the County government (without finances from the State) would allow such a thing to happen.

But that didn't stop Bill from praying fervently! In my conversations with him, he assured me he prayed every day about this matter. And he called and wrote anyone he thought could help. He finally received a listening ear from our United States Congressman at the time, Burt Talcott, who agreed the road posed a real threat to safety. His voice received some hearing in county and state circles, but the problem continued unresolved. Bill added:

> Adding insult to injury, some of our neighbors decided not to support us. They misunderstood our motives, thinking all we were interested in was 'peace and quiet' on the conference grounds. But it went far beyond that motive. We needed a safe situation for 60,000 annual Mount Hermon guests, 500 tax-paying residents and thousands of passersby.[3]

It seemed evident the only way to get a new bypass was for someone or something to close the old road. But what was the likelihood of that?

Bill enlisted hundreds of Mount Hermon residents and friends to pray along with him, trusting the promise the Lord made to His disciples two thousand years before:

> ...truly I say to you, if you have faith as a mustard seed, you shall say to this mountain, 'Move from here to there' and it shall move; and nothing shall be impossible to you.
> —Matthew 17:20

Conference Drive had

Late 1968 was a particularly wet winter season, characterized by a series of heavy rainstorms. They were powerful enough to temporarily close Mount Hermon Road with mudslides. Eventually road crews repaired the damage and the road re-opened. Bill then saw that if Mount Hermon Road could be closed due to some major "natural phenomenon," there may be a possible solution to the dilemma they faced. The government would be forced to create an alternative highway—the Mount Hermon Bypass! He set out to pray toward that end. "Ask and it shall be given unto you," the Scriptures promised.

One spring night in 1969—as Bill ended the day on his knees beside his bed—he prayed, "Lord, why not tonight?" He was specifically asking the Lord for something dramatic and supernatural to close down that road.

And that's exactly what the Lord did!

During the night, eight inches of rain drenched Mount Hermon. And God took out that road. The north end of Mount Hermon Road, far enough out not to impact any of the conference center properties, lay a river of mud and debris. Bill reports:

I was absolutely ecstatic. There were trees, underbrush, telephone poles, chunks of asphalt, and dirt everywhere. The pavement was fractured. In one area the road had dropped two feet. Mount Hermon Road was now totally impassable. And it was eerily quiet. Gone was the roar of traffic. Gone were all the trucks and cars.

It appeared the road was gone for good. For the first time in the history of the camp we could now walk back and forth to facilities in peace and safety without dodging traffic.

The best part about it all was that our prayers were answered by a direct act of God. [4]

Visiting the slide, March 1969

Author and longtime constituent, Kay Gudnason, further described the scene in *Rings in the Redwoods*:

> *Ledges opened up like those of an earthquake. Mount Hermon Road was choked with a mass of mud, rocks, trees, and debris. Only a footpath was negotiable and the road was closed. Children rode bicycles, squirrels bounded leisurely and people crossed at will without mounting the overpass or observing the crosswalk. This act...speeded the process of decision and acted as a catalyst to bring into motion actions that could otherwise never have been expected.* [5]

Now it was up to the county of Santa Cruz to address and fix the situation. A temporary detour was constructed while options were explored for a permanent solution. Lack of funding for the repair was the biggest problem at that point.

Congressman Talcott had been working diligently behind the scenes in Washington, D.C. and later that spring informed the government of Santa Cruz County that he had secured a $2.1 million federal appropriation in order to build the bypass!

Indeed, God was at work. He heard our prayers and provided in ways only He could bring to pass.

In my years at Mount Hermon, I have heard and told this story many times, but I never tire of it. I still take people to the end of Conference Drive just past our property line where the mudslide occurred. It starts with a berm of earth now grown up with small trees, brush, and weeds. Much of the damage is now overgrown, but you can still see chunks of the road, far from where they once were built. Some are more than fifty feet down in the Bean Creek canyon. That God would move a mountain in order to protect our grounds is such a testimony to His love and faithfulness for Mount Hermon. He listened and answered when we prayed.

By the way, we weren't the only ones in the community who recognized this was God's doing. An editorial written February 26, 1969 in The Valley Press reiterated the same thing:

> There is a perfectly logical reason for the giant hill slipping down onto Mount Hermon Road and closing it at the Kaiser Sand and Gravel plant. It has nothing to do with underground springs, earth fissures, or pressures, I say.
>
> I contend it is all those Mount Hermon residents employing their "faith to move mountains" prayer program.[6]

Every once in awhile, the press gets it right!

On July 12, 1972, the first cars were officially allowed to travel the new by-pass, called Mount Hermon Road. "Old" Mount Hermon Road was renamed Conference Drive. Once it was closed to through traffic, Mount Hermon took on a vastly different look and feel. The Conference Center was now much more peaceful and safe. The summer of 1973 was known as the "summer of calm and quiet."

As a wonderful postscript to this story, several years after God moved the mountain, Corrie ten Boom was invited to Mount Hermon to speak at the annual banquet. Her inspirational testimony of surviving the Nazis during World War II is best known through her book *The Hiding Place*. She spent the day at Mount Hermon and as her host, Bill Gwinn gave her a tour of the grounds. And, of course, once he got to the end of Conference Drive, he recounted the story of God moving the mountain in answer to our prayers.

Bill remembered the day very well:

> *Corrie loved the flowers and thought Ponderosa Lodge was impressive, yet she took no photographs that day. As we walked to the slide area, I told her the story of the road, the rain, and what happened that night after praying for years and years.*
>
> *She pulled out her camera and snapped a shot. "Why are you taking a picture of this?" I asked.*
>
> *"Because only God could do that!"* [7]

The rerouting of Mount Hermon Road is one of the most amazing events to take place during the administration of Bill Gwinn. In March of 1978, Bill moved on after twenty-one years as Executive Director. Our constituents missed him greatly. He was such a vital part of all the growth that occurred at Mount Hermon during those years. Naturally, his shoes were hard to fill.

Director Ed Hayes with the planning committee

— • • • —

In a search that lasted over a year, Dr. Edward L. Hayes was named as Mount Hermon's second Executive Director in 1979. Ed came from an academic background at Denver Seminary, so his leadership style and skills were different than Bill's. Under Ed's direction the Child Care Center was completed, two units of Lakeside Lodge were built, and the massive dining hall construction project was finished.

Ed loved the natural beauty of Mount Hermon and volunteered to lead many of the nature hikes that were scheduled during the conference season. A gifted artist, he captured the essence of the area in his pencil and ink drawings, later printed and made into note cards, post cards, and posters.

Ed faithfully served as Executive Director for thirteen years before accepting the position as President of Denver Seminary in November 1992. That's when my family's story intersects with Mount Hermon.

I've shared a great deal about others hearing from Heaven. Let me give you a little background on how the Williams family specifically heard from Heaven before we came to Mount Hermon and I accepted the position as the third Executive Director.

CHAPTER EIGHT

Why Stop Trusting Him Now?

Why do you call me, 'LORD, LORD,'
and do not do what I say?

LUKE 6:46 (NIV)

EVERYONE WHO HAS EVER GONE INTO VOCATIONAL CHRISTIAN MINISTRY HAS A UNIQUE STORY OF GOD'S LEADING. It is the clear and profound conviction that God is specifically calling you to follow Him that is essential to change our values, concentrate our thinking, build necessary trust, and provide needed courage to enter into a new life focus that is often largely unknown. The Williams family has just such a story that first led us into ministry. And we were in camping ministry nearly a dozen years before He brought us to Mount Hermon.

I was born in Altoona, Pennsylvania, but our family moved to Michigan when I was seven years old. Dad pastored a college church right off the campus of Michigan State University. Once I was a teen, I spent my summers working on the summer staff at Camp-of-the-Woods in Speculator, New York, starting out as a lifeguard and quickly working my way to cashier in the accounting office and ultimately to Summer Staff Director.

I was privileged to work closely during those years with the Camp-of-the-Woods' Executive Director, Gordon Purdy. When Gordon was a young man on the Camp-of-the-Woods staff, the Director died suddenly and Gordon was appointed to fill that position.

PREVIOUS Roger with his parents at Gull Lake Bible Conference

By the time I worked on summer staff, Gordon had been Director for nearly fifty years. What a wealth of experience he had to share.

He took a special interest in me. To this day I am grateful for the way he affirmed me, mentored me encouraged my gifts, and communicated confidence in my abilities. He watched me do my work and then together in the late evenings we took time for his favorite night-time snack, Puffed Wheat and fresh peaches. To this day I love that combination because of the wonderful memories it brings back! We talked over the events of the day and he offered helpful counsel and perspective. When I eventually took the position at Mount Hermon, Gordon was so proud, and couldn't resist a little humor. "Let me know to whom I send the bill, Roger," he joked. "Mount Hermon needs to pay me a consulting fee for all the time I spent teaching you the ropes in camping ministry!"

When I graduated from East Lansing High School, I went on to Michigan State University having received a full-ride scholarship and majored in communication and pre-law. Over the Christmas holidays in my junior year, I attended InterVarsity's annual Missions Conference in Urbana, Illinois, mostly to spend time with my Camp-of-the-Woods friends who were also going to be there. During the conference God clearly showed me he wasn't Lord of my pre-law, career-in-politics plans. The verse in Luke 6:46 brought deep conviction and change to my mind and heart.

"Why do you call Me, 'Lord, Lord' and do not do what I say?"

Given my typical Type A, strong "Driver" personality, I was preparing my future plans and giving them to the Lord to "sign and approve." On the final night of that conference, spending hours wandering in a nearby cemetery while snow fell, He made it powerfully clear that was not the way He operated with those He loved and redeemed. He authored the plans. He didn't just sign off on our wild ideas!

I remember wrestling with Him for about four hours until I gave up and asked Him to take charge of everything. I came back to campus with a very different focus; I clearly sensed God calling me into Kingdom ministry–yet I didn't yet know which specific vocation it was (e.g. pastor, missionary, Christian school teacher, etc.).

I was awarded a year-long Rotary Fellowship to Britain later that year and when I filled out the application two years prior, I was expecting to study the history of constitutional law after graduation from Michigan State. As only God can orchestrate, I was awarded my second choice of graduate schools—Edinburgh University in Scotland—the only school of the five I had chosen that had a seminary with a number of strong evangelical professors. Instead of Cambridge, where I had intended to study law with a goal toward politics, I spent an incredibly wonderful year at New College in Edinburgh, Scotland, studying theology in a lecture hall that had a window facing the stern visage of John Knox peering down from a statue in the courtyard!

While working on staff at Camp-of-the-Woods the summer of 1969 (before I left for Scotland), I grew in love with Rachel Anderson from Bemidji, Minnesota. She had a deep love for the Lord, an endearing transparent honesty, a love of the outdoors coupled with a "sporty" and competitive personality, and the most exquisite singing voice I had ever heard. We wrote to each other while I studied overseas and then both returned to Camp-of-the-Woods the summer of 1970. Under a full moon in July, on a far cove of the lake, I asked her to marry me. She said "YES!" We were married eleven months later, June 12, 1971. My father and Gordon Purdy officiated at the marriage ceremony, on the exact date when 26 years before, my dad had married his bride—my mother, It was always wonderful to celebrate our mutual June 12 anniversaries through the years.

In September of 1970 I took a position at Trinity Seminary in Deerfield, Illinois as the Assistant Director of Public Relations, specifically focused on building and deepening relationships with supporting churches. The skills I learned in that position would serve me well in many of my future posts. I worked there for two years until the spring of 1972 when I returned to graduate school at Michigan State. In the fall of 1973, an intriguing opportunity surfaced. Congressman John Dellenback of Oregon's 4TH District invited me to Washington, D.C for an interview. The Congressman, a dedicated Christian, asked me to pray about this before I could give him all the reasons why this wouldn't work. It's hard to tell a Congressman you refuse to pray about something! And wouldn't you know it, God spoke clearly to Rachel and me, directing us eastward to consider this opportunity. We had heard from Heaven!

I had met Congressman Dellenback and some of his staff years earlier through one of the Congressional Prayer Breakfasts I had been involved with during college. He invited me to work for him as one of his legislative assistants. I accepted the position (Rachel was hired by Congressman John Erlenborn of Illinois as a constituent caseworker) and we look back fondly on those heady days in the nation's capitol. It was in the midst of the Watergate scandal, but the government officials we met who genuinely loved the Lord and faithfully attended Bible studies on "the hill" greatly encouraged us. We both worked for congressmen for two and a half years until Congressman Dellenback lost his bid for re-election to a fifth term in 1976. We tearfully said our good-byes to the wonderful friends we made there (including Alden and Lorna Johanson). At the time, who would have guessed that we'd have the joy of working together at Mount Hermon thirty years later?! Now we sought the Lord's direction for His next assignment.

We decided to move back to Michigan with the hope that I could further my graduate studies at Michigan State, but we also had to eat and pay the rent. So I went to work for a business called Computer Sciences Corporation, where I managed the marketing team for the next six years. Eventually I was overseeing a six-state territory in the Upper Midwest.

From a human perspective, this was a wonderful season in our lives. I was moving up the corporate ladder in a very successful company and earning a handsome salary. By then we had been blessed with our first child, Sara. And we were able to build the house of our dreams, one we intended to use like Francis and Edith Schaeffer used L'Abri, as a place available for open spiritual discussions with students from Michigan State. We were plugged into a wonderful church, led weekly Bible studies, and were members of the choir. I was convinced I could be a Christian in the marketplace, and enjoyed the challenge of influencing people in their search for the Lord while making the kind of money that would allow us to give generously to ministries around the world.

"Were we using our time to the greatest advantage for His Kingdom?"

During those business years, I agreed to serve on the Board of Camp Barakel, one of the two largest camps in the State of Michigan. My father had been a speaker for several of the fall Deer Hunting Camps and taken me with him, so I was acquainted with the ministry and excited to be part of its future planning.

Even though we were deeply involved in ministry, Rachel and I found ourselves increasingly uneasy during this time of material success. The Lord kept bringing us back to a singular question: Were we using our time to the greatest advantage for His Kingdom? Honestly, we felt we were doing all we could to serve the Lord as highly committed lay people. The pressure of this question puzzled us for months until we found ourselves becoming more and more uncomfortable. "What is it You have in mind for us, Lord?" we asked. There was only silence.

On January 31, 1981, God gave us His answer on our way back from a Camp Barakel Board meeting. Rachel and I have always enjoyed driving together and chatting about whatever comes to our minds. We were about forty minutes from home in Eaton Rapids when I decided to bring up "the issue" once again.

"Hon, we've been wondering for nearly thirteen months what God wants to do with our lives. Yet He has never answered or provided direction. We've been met with silence. What if it's something totally outside of anything we've ever thought of? Are you ready to give up our house?" I was certain that would be too much to ask of her since she had helped to design it, had stones from her birthplace in the living room fireplace and had designed decorator spaces for all our antique furniture. I was sure she would decline—or at least ask for some time to pray and consider. She responded instantly, and her answer was heartfelt and surprising.

She looked at me. "Rog, it's just a thing. I want to be in the center of God's will and if He wants us to move, that's what I want! Let's put the sign up tonight!"

I looked at her in disbelief.

"I'm serious," she went on. "Let's hang a 'For Sale' sign in the front yard tonight."

I've always had deep respect for Rachel, but this awed me. It was obvious she was further down the "trust" road than I was.

"Let me ask you a question," she returned. "Are you ready to give up your job?"

I really didn't want to answer that question. At that moment my honest answer was "No." I loved my job I loved my staff. I loved my boss. I loved my income. However, at that exact moment, the same words that had confronted me years ago from Luke 6: 46 came crashing back into my consciousness:

Why do you call Me 'Lord, Lord'
and do not do what I say?

I looked over at Rachel, "I certainly don't feel like saying, 'Yes.' But if He's Lord, and that is what He wants, the only answer I can give is 'Yes.' Otherwise He's not really the Lord of my life!"

That was a monumental turning point and both of us knew it. Together we prayed, although I did keep my eyes open since I was driving! I can still see that spot on the highway where this happened. Today I call it our A-cubed prayer: anything, anywhere, anytime. We told the Lord we were available for whatever He wanted, whenever, and wherever. Little did we know that God would begin showing us almost immediately what He wanted.

We had been home only a couple of hours when we heard a knock on the front door. (I'm not making this up!) Standing there was the Director of Camp Barakel, Dave Johnson. We had just left him less than three hours before, and he said nothing about heading in our direction. I wondered what this visit could be about.

"Come in, Dave!" I led him to the living room where we sat down. "What's up? Is everything OK?" His usual cheerful expression was missing.

"For years I've been praying about a new director for Camp Barakel," he blurted. "Three weeks ago—after eight years of praying—God answered my prayer. It needs to be a person with—," and then he proceeded for twenty minutes to list the attributes and qualities the camp needed in a new director.

He was the director, wasn't he? Why was he telling me this?

He saw the questions on my face. He said he knew I probably was unaware that when his dad, Johnny Johnson, founder and first director, had to step down due to health issues, he had been asked to come back to "fill in" with the understanding the Board would immediately begin looking for a new director. For years he'd filled in. He never felt called to be the director, but the Board liked him and suspended its search. I had no idea of that history.

"Three weeks ago God showed me who this person should be," Dave concluded.

"Who?" I asked, still in the dark. I was honored he had come to seek my counsel as a Board member regarding this individual.

"It's YOU!" he said as he pointed his finger at me. I was completely speechless. My lips moved but no words came out.

"What did you just say?" Rachel's voice sounded from the hall. She had just finished putting our daughter to bed and had caught the tail end of the conversation.

> *"I call it our A³ Prayer: anything, anywhere, anytime."*

Hurrying into the living room, she looked me squarely in the eye. "Rog, do you realize *about three hours ago* we told God we would be available to be used any way He wanted? Anywhere. Anytime. Wow! We can't ignore Dave's offer. We need to seriously consider this possibility."

My heart finally stopped pounding, I caught my breath, and my voice returned. The three of us ended up talking late into the night. About four o'clock in the morning, we agreed to begin praying earnestly about the offer, and then fell into bed, exhausted.

After Dave left the next morning, Rachel and I agreed not to discuss it any further for the following week, but to pray separately, waiting for God to bring us to the same conclusion. We heard nothing from Heaven. So we agreed to pray for a second week.

In the middle of that second week we hosted our regular Tuesday night couples Bible study. I was responsible for leading the discussion and began by reading from Ephesians 5, verses 15–16:

"Be very careful, then, how you live—not as unwise
but as wise, making the most of every opportunity, because
the days are evil."

I felt like I'd been hit with a ton of bricks. In that moment, I heard from Heaven! The Holy Spirit clearly assured me this was God's plan for us. This was our opportunity to enter the "front lines" of full-time ministry. I had my answer. I could hardly wait for the Bible study to end so I could talk with Rach. "I have to talk with you!" I whispered in her ear as the couples were going out the front door.

"Me, too," she replied softly.

"We're not giving up anything... We're being promoted!"

The minute the door closed, we turned to each other. "Tonight God absolutely confirmed in my heart that He wants us to go to Barakel." Holding my breath, I waited for her to respond.

"God has been impressing me with the same thought during my prayer times this week, but I thought we had to finish the week out before talking about it!" she said and smiled.

We hugged each other, thanked God, and called Dave to share the news. As long as I live I will never forget his response:

"You're...you're willing to give up all you have?"

"Gladly," I replied. "Thank you for helping us think about something we would never have considered in our wildest dreams."

"Are you *sure* you want to give up everything?" he probed.

"We're not giving up anything," I replied. "We're being promoted!"

Roger and Rachel with Sara, just before they accepted the call to Camp Barakel

The following day I spoke with my boss about our new life direction. Being a wonderful Christian man, he shared the excitement of our decision but asked me to remain in my position for another six months so that I could help train my successor. I agreed.

The next thing on our list was to put our house up for sale. But a deep recession had hit Michigan during that year of 1981. We knew it would be difficult to sell a large home in a depressed economy.

For the next six months we did not receive even one nibble. Finally we needed to move to Barakel. We packed up our belongings and left our vacant dream house, hoping it would sell even though we wouldn't be in the area.

"You've trusted God throughout your life, and throughout all these recent, life-changing decisions. Why stop trusting Him now?"

Barakel's staff were not paid salaries, but lived on the gracious financial support of friends and churches, which meant we also needed to "raise support." By the time we moved in November, God had provided our monthly needs through the friends in the three couples' Bible studies we had started, as well as our church, but there was nothing "extra" for monthly mortgage payment on the house in Eaton Rapids. We dipped into our small savings account in order to make the payments. We had pretty much drained our savings when we built and paid cash for most of the construction costs. Our residual account was declining quickly. Early in April 1982 we reached a crisis point.

Not knowing who else to turn to, I picked up the phone and called my dad. He had always been supportive when I needed counsel, so perhaps he could help me figure out what to do.

"How are you doing, Son?" Dad asked from the other end of the line.

"I need your advice, Dad," I confessed. "We have enough money in our savings account to make one more payment on the house in May, and then I don't know what we'll do. I've never defaulted or not fulfilled an agreement in my life—kinda goes against my grain. However, I'm not sure what's going on. I talked with my old boss and he said he would take me back in a minute if that's what I decided to do. Is this God's way of telling us we've made a mistake by going into camping ministry? Should I go back to business?"

After a pause, Dad responded, "Son, you've trusted God throughout your life, and throughout all these recent, life-changing decisions. Why stop trusting Him now?"

I hung up the phone knowing he was absolutely right. There was no reason to stop trusting the Lord, no matter how bleak our circumstances appeared. It was as if I were re-living what the first Mount Hermon Board of Directors faced when they declared, "We will go on, in the dark, trusting God."

The day after I had that conversation with my dad, I received a phone call from a former business competitor. He wasn't aware of what was happening in our lives so I shared about my new role as director of Camp Barakel. After some casual conversation, he broached the real reason for his call.

"So I guess the rumor I've heard about you trying to sell your Eaton Rapids house is true. Is it still for sale?"

"As a matter of fact, it is," I replied, trying my best to remain calm.

"Can I go see it?" he pressed.

"Right now?"

"Yes."

"Well sure! The neighbor next door has a key. I'll let her know you'll be coming by. Take all the time you need." Rachel and I spent the next hours praying, on pins and needles until he called back the next morning.

"We love the house. We'd like to buy it."

"That's wonderful!" Could I believe the words I was hearing?

"And if it's okay with you," he continued a bit facetiously, "rather than going through a bank or mortgage company, I'd like to pay in full...with cash!"

After I caught my breath, I shared the details of my conversation with my dad the previous day. Then he was astonished. So I asked what was on my mind. "Would it be possible to close by the twentieth of May? That way I won't miss any of my mortgage payments."

"Hum," he hesitated. "That's a little faster than I anticipated, but I think we can make it happen. Let me see what we can do!"

We closed May 15TH.

Only God! Why had I questioned Him in the first place? He obviously loved us and could be trusted to take care of us.

Why stop trusting Him now?

It is a lesson He continues to teach me.

NINE

Hearing From Heaven Half-way Around the World

Jabez cried out to the God of Israel, "Oh, that you would bless me and enlarge my territory! Let your hand be with me, and keep me from harm so that I will be free from pain." And God granted his request.

I CHRONICLES 4:10 (NIV)

BY NOW IT'S BECOMING EVIDENT THAT THE MINISTRY OF MOUNT HERMON… AND THE CONCEPT OF "HEARING FROM HEAVEN…" ARE INTIMATELY WOVEN TOGETHER. Dr. Gilchrist heard from Heaven and the idea for Mount Hermon was born. The first Board of Directors heard from Heaven, and progress continued despite a massive earthquake. Cliff Barrows heard from Heaven at the age of eleven and committed his life to Christ at Redwood Camp. Richard Halverson heard from Heaven and gave his life to full-time ministry as a young adult at Victory Circle.

I'm sure you've heard from Heaven, as well. You don't have to be famous or a certain age to hear from Heaven if you're following the Lord. Rachel and I know this personally as we have some similar stories. One of the best has to do with how we came to Mount Hermon.

After six years of my directing Camp Barakel in northern Michigan, we moved east to America's Keswick in New Jersey where I served as Director for four years. Then came the invitation from Gull Lake Bible Conference near Kalamazoo, Michigan. The thought of returning to my home state energized us. It was there my parents and sister and I spent many summers enjoying family conferences

PREVIOUS Roger at his desk in Mount Hermon 1993

during my "growing up" years. We all loved this ministry. At Gull Lake I learned many of the stories in the Bible from Tim LaHaye's mother, Margaret. I also learned to swim as a child. What an honor it was to be invited to return as Director. We heard from Heaven, said "yes" to the Lord, and arrived in June of 1992. By then I had been in camping leadership for a little over a decade.

In November of that same year, Dr. Ed Hayes, executive director at Mount Hermon, announced his resignation. The Board of Directors immediately formed a search committee to find the next Executive Director. Their first order of business was to send a letter to a number of leaders in the Christian camping world asking them to nominate people for the position. Included with the letter was a list with the title *The Twenty Desired Characteristics for Mount Hermon's Executive Director*. It was comprehensive and broad in scope.

I was one of the people selected to receive that letter and after praying about it, I nominated two persons I thought could accomplish the enormous task of running a ministry of Mount Hermon's magnitude. Within the next few weeks, four or five of my camping colleagues began calling me, asking if they could nominate me for the position. That was so unexpected! I honestly felt it was a job for a camping "Superstar," and I've never harbored any delusions about my being in that category.

"Thank you for the affirmation," I told each one, "but please don't. Mount Hermon is far too significant a ministry to place my name in nomination. It's a position for the person that has clearly heard from Heaven. I've heard nothing from the Lord about a change in ministry location."

"But, Rog..."

"Please, listen to me. I am less than a year into my new role here at Gull Lake, I'm very happy and challenged, and in light of my just accepting this position, I don't even think it's appropriate to discuss it. Thanks for thinking of me, however."

Early in May I received another call, but this time it was not from one of my camping friends.

"Hello, Roger. My name is Gil Sheffield and I am the chairman of the Search Committee for the Executive Director position at Mount Hermon."

Somewhat shocked, I answered, "Good afternoon."

Gil continued. "Do you have time to answer three questions?"

"Yes, of course," I replied, though guarded.

"Roger, your name has been placed in nomination for this position by several camping leaders and yet I understand you don't want your name to stand. Can you tell me why?" The non-verbal cues were curiously laced with wariness...was I hiding something like being a bank robber or horse thief?

I took a few deep breaths. "Gil, Mount Hermon is too major and too important a ministry in Christian camping for someone just to throw his name 'in the hat.' Any person coming to you needs to have directly heard from Heaven that the Lord wants him to apply. Frankly, I haven't heard a thing!" I'm not sure I had even prayed about this opportunity. It didn't seem right since I had just come to Gull Lake as Director.

"Thank you," Gil responded. "My second question: Do you believe the words of Psalm 37 that state 'the steps of a good man are ordered by the Lord'?"

"I certainly do," I answered. "I support that thesis."

"Then my third question...why won't you allow God to order your steps?"

I felt graciously rebuked. As you know, I had never prayed about the position, fully assuming God had someone else in mind. Perhaps God might be asking me to consider the issue, so I backed off a bit and told him I would begin to pray about it.

With the door open just a crack, Gil pushed a little harder. "That's wonderful, Roger. Now, would you please send me your resume?"

"No, Gil. Not until I've heard from Heaven."

I could sense Gil dialing down his persistence a notch or two. "You know, Roger, it would be a big help to me personally if you would send me your resume. There are a number of people who've placed your name in nomination and I'm sensing a fair amount of pressure from the committee. It would be a big favor to me."

"Okay, Gil." I acquiesced. "I'll send my resume based on your request as a friend. But please understand four qualifications. First, I am *not interested* in this position. I will only be interested if I hear something from the Lord. I am sending my resume as a favor to you. Second, I'm going to call my Gull Lake Board President and let him know about our conversation. Third, you will assure your committee that I am not a candidate. And finally, you will not call me in five days for an interview." Gil agreed to each of these.

With those stipulations in place, I put my resume, as requested, in express mail.

Five days later, Gil Sheffield called for an interview.

"Hi Roger, it's Gil. What are you doing this Saturday?"

"Why are you asking?"

"Well (long pause) we began our search with approximately 180 names and we have now boiled it down to a short list of seven candidates—and you're one of the seven. We're hoping to interview each candidate, preferably all on the same day. Could you meet with us this Saturday?"

"Gil, your job just got one seventh easier," I answered. "You know I'm not a candidate. And this Saturday I'm leading our first Single Parent Family Conference at Gull Lake. I'll be busy from eight in the morning until midnight."

"So, no chance of seeing you Saturday?" he persisted.

"No."

"All right. Here's how you could help us, then," Gil continued. (In retrospect, I honestly think he was making this up as he was going along, but God certainly used it!) "Could you come in Friday night and let us practice our interview questions on you? You could critique and help refine our questions in preparation for the other candidates' interviews."

"That's creative!" I replied. "You didn't have a lot of time to think that up!"

"You're right." Gil laughed.

"All kidding aside," I went on, "if I can help, I will. I have such respect for the ministry of Mount Hermon, and I have quite a bit of interviewing experience from both business and camping leadership. Let me see if I can find someone here at Gull Lake to sub for me Friday night. But I'll need you to find me a 'red-eye' flight that will get me back here by seven o'clock Saturday morning."

"I'll get on it right away. Thanks, Roger."

We hung up and I went to work finding my sub for Friday. Actually, I went home to ask Rachel to step in for me since I was the entire program department at Gull Lake! After some discussion, she finally agreed to kick off the conference in my absence. In the amount of time it took to talk her into it, Gil had called back to tell me my flights had been arranged and he would pick me up at the San Jose Airport late Friday afternoon.

I'm glad he told me what airport I was flying into, because up to that point I had no idea where Mount Hermon was located. I knew it was in California, but beyond that, I was clueless. California is a huge state!

As promised, Gil met me Friday at the airport and whisked me off to dinner at a nearby hotel with the four other members of the Search Committee. We had a delightful time of fellowship around the table. By seven o'clock we began the interview/critiquing process in a private conference room. Each person asked a question, I answered, and when all five had finished, they began a new round of questions. We went around the circle four times.

Finally, after glancing at my watch, I realized I had only twenty-five minutes left for critiquing before I needed to grab the cab to get back to the airport. I interrupted their questioning and began reviewing, offering what I considered to be helpful critiques—and suggested rephrasing—of some of their questions. Their looks of shock and astonishment caught me off guard. They were speechless.

Out of the corner of my eye I saw Gil get up from his chair and stand behind the other four committee members, giving me a look that said, "They didn't know you were going to critique them."

It was an awkward moment, but I plowed on. I didn't want to fail them after accepting the responsibility for being part of the process. I concluded my remarks, and promised to pray that God would bring the right person to direct Mount Hermon, thanked them for dinner and for the privilege of meeting them. We shook hands...and "I got out of Dodge!"

Three weeks later, I woke up at seven o'clock on a Saturday morning to get ready for the events that were part of our Memorial Day Weekend Family Conference at Gull Lake. Gifted communicator Tony Campolo was our speaker and we were packed out. Our guests and staff were so excited and so was I—not only about the conference, but also on the Monday following the conference a group of us were leaving for a three-week short-term evangelism/church planting mission project in the Ukraine.

At the request of the Ukrainian Baptist Union, Gull Lake was sending nine of our summer staff college musicians along with me to put on concerts, speak in schools, orphanages and factories, engage in street evangelism, and do whatever we could to clearly and lovingly share the Gospel with the Ukrainian people.

As mentioned, that Saturday morning our home phone rang at seven o'clock. Was something amiss? My mind went on alert. Maybe ovens were down, or there was guest health emergency, or a fire in the child care building. As the Camp Director I'd be the first one called.

"Hello?"

"Hi Roger—it's Gil Sheffield. Do you have a pen?"

"Gil, why are you calling at four o'clock your time to ask me if I have a pen?" But I admit I had a good hunch why he was calling.

"Rog, I need fourteen references from you."

"What for?"

"We've narrowed the seven names down to three candidates and you are one of the three finalists."

"Please stop right there, Gil," I interrupted. "As I told you before, I'm not a candidate. I'm only a nominee because someone I don't know put my name on your list. But I can't be considered a genuine candidate until I hear from Heaven, which still hasn't happened. And I've been praying every day since your first call!"

"Relax, Roger, relax," Gil replied. "Can I get those names from you as one of our nominees?"

I had to make some quick decisions. "Okay, Gil. Here's what I'll do. First of all, it's essential that you keep this confidential. This is the seventy-fifth anniversary year for Gull Lake and I don't want rumors diminishing any of the enthusiasm surrounding the celebration. Do you promise not to say a word about this?"

"Yes," Gil replied.

"Second, the Christian camping community is a small and fairly tight-knit group. If you use the word 'candidate' in your phone calls, I'll hear about it. And so will the folks at Gull Lake Bible Conference. Promise to only use the word 'nominee' when you gather whatever information you desire. And, I'll state it again. I'll only consider this position if—and only if—I hear something from Heaven. Otherwise the answer is 'no.' Are we in agreement on this?"

"Yes."

"All right then. I'll send you fourteen references but no names from Gull Lake."

"Fine! Could those fourteen names stem from your previous camp and business experiences? We're looking specifically for the names of three people at each location who saw you as an effective leader and one who thought you weren't effective."

This sounded like a wise approach so I agreed. Quietly, I also decided I would speak to the whole Executive Committee of the Board at Gull Lake since I never wanted them to hear about these conversations "through the back door."

"Thank you, Roger. We'll be in touch. What's the best time to talk with you over the next few weeks?"

"How's your Russian?" I joked.

"What?"

"How's your Russian? In two days I leave for three weeks in the Ukraine. Our schedule is somewhat fluid depending on the attitudes of local authorities. The only phone number I can give you is for the central office of the Ukrainian Baptist Union in Kiev, but they only have an English speaking person available about 10% of the time."

"Hmmm," Gil grumbled.

The trip to the Ukraine was fantastic. Our little team had the privilege of watching God make an eternal impact on thousands of those precious people—men and women who had never heard of God's unconditional love or His sending His Son to be our Savior. Many had never even heard the name of Jesus! The Soviet government had so censored any public religious meetings, books and publications, that most of the population knew nothing of the Bible. It was so exciting to share the Gospel with them. I remember talking to a doctoral candidate in physics who thanked me for bringing the news of salvation in Jesus to her and her people. She told me that night she had become a follower of Jesus. She knew from her research there had to be a God—and now she knew His name.

Each morning we rose early (around 5:30 a.m.) and jumped on board our mini-bus for the journey to the day's many ministry venues. We started most days in schools, factories and orphanages, and ended our four to six concert/speaking day to packed crowds in the cities' civic centers (called "Palaces of Culture") with mosaics of Vladimir Lenin staring down at us as we shared the Good News of Jesus Christ. In those early mornings, I made a habit of sitting near the back row of the bus using the travel time for prayer.

I recalled that in December of 1992, the vice-president of our Gull Lake Board had encouraged me to pray the prayer of Jabez every day during 1993. He committed to do the same. I'm sure you're familiar with Jabez' prayer in I Chronicles 4:10:

> *Oh that You would bless me and enlarge my territory!*
> *Let Your Hand be with me and keep me from harm so that I*
> *will be free from pain.*

The Board had just voted to purchase land adjacent to our conference center that doubled the acreage for Gull Lake. As a Board, we were considering a number of ministry options to develop our new property. This prayer, with its multiple requests—1) bless us, 2) enlarge our territory, 3) keep Your Hand on us, and 4) keep us free from pain (foolish decisions)—seemed the perfect prayer to pray in light of our "enlarged territory" with its many options.

Around 6:30 a.m. on Monday morning during the second week of our trip, I was sitting in the back of the mini-bus praying the prayer of Jabez as it related to Gull Lake. At that moment in my prayer, I heard someone speaking to me.

I want to talk with you about enlarging your territory.

I don't regularly hear God communicating audibly (although it has happened at other turning points in my life) so I turned around to see if someone was behind me. There was no one. "Is it You, Lord?" I asked.

I don't want you to be the one to expand Gull Lake's territory. I want to take your family to California, to Mount Hermon.

I immediately became frustrated. If this was really the Lord, why was He interrupting my "Gull Lake prayer" to talk to me about Mount Hermon? Why couldn't He wait until I prayed about Mount Hermon later in my morning prayer time? Looking back I can't believe my audacity. Here I was fussing about my process with the Lord of the Universe. I was so frustrated, I concluded my prayer right there with a pronounced "Amen."

Later I wondered if I'd been imagining things. "If it happens again tomorrow, I'll know it's from the Lord," I muttered under my breath. With that, I rejoined the crew at the front of the mini-bus.

On Tuesday, it happened again. Same time at the back of the mini-bus, as I prayed for Gull Lake.

Let Me try again, Roger. I don't want you to be the one to expand Gull Lake. I want to take your family to California.

Now I knew it was the Lord speaking to me. I was both amazed and perplexed. "I'm not prepared to talk about that right now," I responded hesitantly. "Perhaps tomorrow." During that Tuesday, my perplexity morphed into the major question I wanted to ask the Lord.

> *"Why do you want to put me, a total stranger, in that role at Mount Hermon?"*

On Wednesday, the voice came again at the same place in my prayer. "Lord, I know that's it You, but I need to ask You something. I don't know a soul in California. I don't know the culture of California. I don't know the history of Mount Hermon. I don't even know where Mount Hermon is located. I know Michigan. I know Gull Lake. I grew up here. I know the culture of the Midwest. I fit here. There are at least thirty million people in California. Surely some of them have attended Mount Hermon. They know its ministry and its history. Why don't you choose one of them? Why do you want to put me, a total stranger, in that role at Mount Hermon?"

I will never forget His penetrating answer.

Because I want to put you in a place so new, so large, so complex that you will not be able to lead in the strength of your personality. You will have to trust Me!

I was stunned. My gracious Lord *really* knew me—knew my shortcomings and was working overtime to "conform me to the image of His Son" (Romans 8:29). Instantly I remembered from a previous time the words of Luke 6:46, "Why do you call me 'Lord, Lord' and do not do what I say?" Suddenly I was humbled and obedient in His presence right there in the back of the bus. "Thank You, Lord, for Your patience and grace in putting up with my frustrations and answering my question. You certainly know me, don't you? I do want You to be my Lord. Completely! We will obey You and go to California."

"We came because we were called by our gracious Lord to this wonderful ministry."

While sitting there, I realized that practically everything in our life was about to change. I needed to get to a phone in order to call Rachel; I needed to share this direct message from the Lord. That was not an easy task in the Ukraine at that time in history. There were very few functional phones available and to call overseas required setting up a reservation with an operator. The whole process usually took about two hours to accomplish. All day Wednesday and Thursday I looked for a working phone with no success. Finally, on Friday while we were having lunch in a Ukrainian home, I spied a phone. I asked our hostess if I could use it. "Certainly," she said, "but you're scheduled to leave here in one hour and fifteen minutes. It usually takes two hours to secure the operator."

"I'd like to try anyway," I answered.

One hour and ten minutes later, the operator called and connected me with Rachel. Before I could even say a word, she exclaimed, "Oh Roger, Roger, Roger, I am so glad you called. I really need to talk to you. But you'll have to sit down!"

I felt panicked. "Are the girls alive?"

"Yes, alive and well." She laughed. "But I think God wants us to go to Mount Hermon."

I was shocked. "No...no...no. I'm calling you to tell you the very same thing. How did this happen?"

"On Monday as I was again praying about it" said Rachel, "and I felt as if the Lord came down and sat on the edge of our bed, put His arm around me and shared that this was our new ministry location for the whole family. I believe I've heard from Heaven."

"That happened Monday?"

"Yes."

"That's the same day I heard from Heaven, too!" I didn't have the courage at that moment to tell her it took me an extra two days of arguing procedural issues with God before I obeyed.

Ten thousand miles apart, on the same day, Rachel and I heard from Heaven. God gave us the same message. *Go to Mount Hermon.*

We arrived with plenty of unanswered questions. But one thing we both knew for certain. We came because we were called by our gracious Lord to this wonderful ministry. We now had heard from Heaven.

TEN

Hearing from Heaven on a Sleepless Night

And whatever you do, whether in word or deed, do it all in the name of the Lord Jesus, giving thanks to God the Father through him.

COLOSSIANS 3:17 (NIV)

ON LABOR DAY OF 1993, I ARRIVED TO BEGIN MY NEW ROLE AT MOUNT HERMON. Our family was settling in, eagerly preparing for a new chapter in our lives. I hit the ground running in my position as Executive Director while our daughters began getting comfortable with their new schools.

There was no official job description when I started at Mount Hermon, so I took the list of "Twenty Desirable Characteristics for the Executive Director" that had been sent out with the search letter and made that the initial basis for establishing my role. It was an exhilarating challenge since the list was very comprehensive.

The Board of Directors assigned me an initial task—to create a Strategic Plan that would encompass the full scope of all the Mount Hermon ministries. It was a major undertaking for someone who had just arrived. I met with the staff of each department in order to summarize what their area of ministry looked like at the time and to get input as to their dreams for the future. It proved to be a great way to get acquainted with these dedicated individuals. We began dreaming together.

The summer Family Camp schedule took priority. We all agreed there needed to be a "break-day," a kind of Sabbath in the middle of

PREVIOUS Roaring Camp Train leaving Redwood Camp during the summer the week. Being the new kid on the block, I raised a question about something I had observed that we could explore.

"Tell me about the railroad tracks down at Redwood Camp," I said.

"They are fully functional," I was told. "On occasion a train from Roaring Camp Railroad uses the tracks through Redwood Camp to transport sand. And the trains across the street take people all the time down to the Santa Cruz Boardwalk from their depot. It goes through the virgin Redwoods of Henry Cowell State Park and along the San Lorenzo River Canyon. It's a beautiful trip."

"Isn't Roaring Camp our neighbor?" I inquired.

"Yes."

"Well, if the railroad runs from 'next door,' why couldn't it back up to us?" I posed. "We could fill the train with our conferees. They'd ride to Santa Cruz, spend the day swimming and playing on the beach, stroll the boardwalk and wharf, and enjoy the rides. We could pack picnic lunches for them to enjoy on the beach."

Everyone liked the idea. So, we made a few calls to Roaring Camp and negotiated a contract to bring the train into Redwood Camp on Wednesdays at 9:30 in the morning. Railroad staff were also willing to bring conferees back from Santa Cruz either on the 12:30 or 4:30 train in the afternoon. It was the perfect midweek break. Instantly it became a favorite activity during our summer weeks.

It's been very gratifying to hear the stories of shared *inter-generational memories* — grandparents mesmerized their grandchildren with their own stories of when train travel was the major way to get from place to place. It was a wonderful way to link families together.

Along with "Train Day" we added the Friday night celebration at Victory Circle—a place for singing and sharing some of the things God accomplished in lives during the week. It seemed so appropriate to include the Lord's Table as another aspect of this special event.

By week's end, the conferees were like family so what better way to end our time together?

———— • • • ————

We also spent a great deal of time thinking through the optimum use of our facilities. Like most camps and conference centers, we often filled our facilities throughout the summer months and almost all the weekends the rest of the year. But the midweek days during the school year were often empty. Wouldn't it be terrific if we could fill our beds all year long? The staff has frequently heard me say, "We can't minister to empty beds." Enter the idea of an Outdoor Science School program.

"Wouldn't it be terrific if we could fill our beds all year long?"

Even a casual glance at the beauty of God's creation around Mount Hermon is awe inspiring. On our four hundred and fifty-five acres, there are a number of distinct ecosystems. If we could help students get a glimpse of the Designer Who created all this beauty, and teach them to be good stewards of these gifts, what a great use of our time that would be. And as we reached out to public (as well as Christian) schools, we would impact thousands of children with whom we'd never have contact otherwise. We would talk about summer camps and perhaps interest a number of them to return for that program. I began asking God to lead us to the right individual to run an Outdoor Science School.

In the spring of 1994 I was down in southern California with Ron Demolar, our Director of Program Ministries, helping another camp with some programming ideas they were curious about. They were also laying the groundwork for an Outdoor Science School, the exact sort of initiative I envisioned as part of our program at

Mount Hermon. Several of us gathered outside the Ontario Airport in a hotel conference room to share ideas and pray.

I was immediately impressed with a man who appeared to be the one that would direct the science school program for that ministry. Rick Oliver's level of understanding and teaching experience regarding a Creator/Designer-based Outdoor Science School program was extensive. He had completed his studies of Evolutionary Biology at the University of California-Irvine and was less than a year away from receiving his Ph.D. Rick's acumen was so respected in the scientific community that he was one of a select few who had been invited to research Mount St. Helens (once it was safe to go in) right after the eruptions in 1980. Rick entered the world of science as a firm evolutionist but came out a believer in the Creator of the universe. He had an amazing story about meeting Jesus as Savior.

All during that day, my respect for Rick increased. I wanted to talk with him about our science school idea. But I didn't want to put him or his camp in an awkward position, nor was it the right thing to do. So during a coffee break I started talking with him, and sharing my desire to start a program at Mount Hermon. I asked if he knew of others with his academic credentials, teaching experience, and heart for ministry who could lead such a program.

Rick smiled broadly and responded, "None that I know of."

"Well, would you keep your eyes open for me, just in case there is another one of you out there?" I begged.

"Sure," he replied.

Can you imagine my excitement when only a few months later Rick Oliver called me on the phone. "Roger, remember our discussion. Would you be interested in me?"

Rick told me the plans for the Outdoor Science School at the camp in southern California had taken a different direction, and to his surprise, he found himself out of a job. He wanted to come to Mount Hermon and was ready to start—the next day.

"Let me talk with a few people and I'll get back to you just as soon as I can," I promised. I figured he'd most likely be making other calls, so if we wanted him we needed to act fast.

The next day I gathered two of my staff members who could best speak to this issue and we sat in my office for several hours, pounding out the pros and the cons of founding an Outdoor Science School program. What would it look like to hire Rick Oliver? What were the implications of that decision? Was there a market for this type of program? Where would the resources come from as we developed the curriculum? I was hoping there'd be a unanimous vote of confidence to hire Rick, but to my surprise, though one man thought it was a good idea, the other felt we should hold off. From his perspective, we needed to do more research and study before plunging ahead. I knew by holding off we would probably miss our window to hire Rick, but chose to honor the fact that we were not all in agreement and ended the meeting.

The rest of the day and evening, all I could do was pray, asking the Lord to help me understand how to make sense of the meeting that had just occurred. The Lord answered by giving me a sleepless night. When I went to bed I tossed and turned. Throughout those long restless hours I continually heard one message from Heaven:

You need to hire Rick Oliver.

It was clear God was giving me His answer. How was I to deal with it in light of my one staff member who wasn't on the same page?

At six o'clock—as the sun rose over the mountain—I took a chance and called my Director of Program Ministries, Ron Demolar, who had participated in the meeting the previous day.

"Ron, did I wake you up?" I asked, knowing he was normally an early riser.

"Actually, I've been up all night," he confessed.

"Why?"

"I went to bed but couldn't sleep. I felt as if God was talking to me all night," he admitted.

"What was He saying?"

"I don't know what you're going to think about this but I kept hearing, *You need to hire Rick Oliver.*

"Well, that makes two of us who couldn't sleep last night. And that's the same message I've been hearing, too!"

That's all I needed to know. The fact that both of us had heard the same message from Heaven was all that mattered. We needed to be operating in sync with how God was directing Mount Hermon. So, even though it wasn't a unanimous decision among our executive staff, we extended an offer to Rick Oliver and he accepted.

The first year Rick was on staff he finished his Ph.D. at UC Irvine while writing the curriculum that we immediately began marketing to schools in our area. Our first Outdoor Science School was held during the fall of 1994 and we haven't looked back.

Over the years, thousands of students have come to Ponderosa Lodge on Monday mornings and spent an amazing five days exploring God's natural beauty under the able instruction of our Christian naturalists. Our instructors do not preach at our public school students, nor jam anything down anyone's throat. But if students or teachers ask questions, we answer freely from our conviction as Christians. All our schools know in advance that we come from a Designer base, not an Evolutionary one.

Dr. Rick Oliver

The theology of nature is a huge issue in today's world. And how you understand God's role is vitally important. If we believe beings are merely accidents of a materialistic evolutionary process—emerging from some primordial ooze—then the worth and dignity of each individual is largely negated and policies supporting abortion, euthanasia, etc. seem entirely appropriate. If, on the other hand, we believe each of us is a unique creation of God—each fashioned in His image (Genesis 1:27)—then of course we will rise to protect and preserve the rights of each individual.

Paul states forcefully in Romans 1:20, "For since the creation of the world God's invisible qualities—his eternal power and divine nature—have been clearly seen, being understood from what has been made, so that men are without excuse." The power of what is seen speaks of a Creator/Designer. We are privileged to share and help thousands of children experience this, and other, Biblical truths through this program.

On Friday mornings, students board the yellow buses and ride back to their schools. And God continues to bring both students and teachers to Himself as a result of learning about His glorious creation. Others come back for summer camp and meet Jesus there. I couldn't be more thrilled with what He's doing through our Outdoor Science School.

Rick Oliver has moved on to his own enlarged ministry of helping others understand the glory of God's creation, but he left us in good hands with trained staff committed to teaching Biblical truth.

How grateful I am that we heard from Heaven and have the privilege of reclaiming some ground for Him!

ELEVEN

I'VE HAD MY MOMENT!

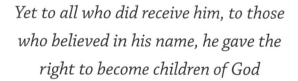

Yet to all who did receive him, to those who believed in his name, he gave the right to become children of God

JOHN 1:12 (NIV)

ONE OF MY GREATEST JOYS DURING MOUNT HERMON'S SUMMER FAMILY CAMPS HAS BEEN THE OPPORTUNITY TO TEACH SEMINARS FOUR DAYS A WEEK. Our typical schedule calls for a main meeting in the auditorium after breakfast, then a refreshment break, complete with homemade donuts, followed by optional seminars geared for parents, married couples, or single parents. We offer a variety of information and activities in these seminars, including nature walks, help with finances, better parenting ideas, in-depth Bible studies, etc. I've been privileged, over the years, to teach Bible studies.

On Monday mornings I normally welcome everyone to the seminar, check to see that the Powerpoint is fully functioning, test my microphone, announce my topic for the week, and launch into my introductory remarks.

But one year something unlikely occurred. While teaching a Monday seminar during the summer of 1996, I was jolted by the appearance of someone sitting on the second row on the right side of the auditorium. It was my sister! I found myself staring at her off and on. What a special treat, I thought to myself. Sis has come all the way from Colorado to surprise me.

PREVIOUS Roger and Rachel teaching during 2013 Creating a Legacy Conference

I found myself spending most of my time speaking to that side of the room, watching her carefully. Whenever we made eye contact, I'd smile and occasionally nod. I even gave her a playful wink now and then.

But she made absolutely no effort to acknowledge me so I looked away. Something was wrong. It slowly dawned on me that this woman might not be my sister—she just looked exactly like Sis. The more I thought about it, the more certain I was that I'd made a huge mistake. I had been staring at this woman. She must have wondered what I was up to! As soon as I finished teaching, I hurried over to introduce myself.

"Hi! I'm Roger Williams and I really need to apologize to you. I have been staring at you throughout my entire seminar and you deserve an explanation. You look exactly like my sister. For half the seminar, I was convinced you were my sister. That's why I was smiling, winking, etc. If I made you uncomfortable, I sincerely apologize."

"That's okay, Roger," the young woman replied. "It's not a problem. I didn't notice, as I was so engrossed in your teaching."

"Thank you. Would you tell me your name?" "I'm Camille Franicevich. My husband, Bob, and I and our two sons, Jack and Tom, are here for our very first Family Camp."

"Well, welcome to Mount Hermon!" I responded. "If you have any questions, or if there is anything I can do to help you have a more enjoyable week, please don't hesitate to ask, okay?"

"Okay," Camille replied with a warm smile. And she was off to pick up Jack and Tom while I chatted briefly with a few more conferees before making my way over to the dining hall for lunch.

After lunch as I strolled back toward my office I heard my name called. I saw Camille approaching from the other direction. "Roger, can I ask you a question?"

"Absolutely. What's up?"

She motioned me to a quiet spot.

Swallowing hard, and looking in each direction, she blurted out in a stage whisper, "Roger, is it all right that we are here? We're Catholics!"

"Oh my goodness, YES!"

Camille seemed to relax.

"Mount Hermon is all about Jesus. And I can tell He's important to you."

"Yes, He is," she answered, the tension in her face subsiding.

"A lot of people don't know this statistic," I explained, "but in our kids' programs at Redwood Camp, for example, most of the children come from 'independent' churches. The second group from Presbyterian churches. And the third from Catholic churches. So please don't feel out of place, Camille. You and your family are very welcome here."

"Thank you, Roger."

"What concerned you?" I pushed a little further.

"We were sitting with another family at lunch and having a nice conversation, getting to know each other. They asked where we came from and we told them we lived in Santa Rosa. After awhile they asked us where we go to church and I explained we attend the Catholic Church in town. They seemed really uncomfortable with that answer."

I again assured her of our absolute delight at having them at Family Camp. After a bit more conversation, we went our separate ways.

Camille and Bob chose separate seminars to attend during that week in order to double the amount of content they received. Camille was faithful in her attendance in my seminar. Every day, she sat in the same spot—to my right on the second row. But as the week came to a close I still had not met Bob.

At my closing seminar on Friday, I took a few minutes to share the importance of having a personal relationship with Jesus.

"Everyone needs to have what I call 'your moment'," I stated. "A time, a date, a place when you know you are trusting in Jesus—and Jesus alone—for your salvation. Your moment has nothing to do with service, tithing, church attendance, Sunday School, etc. It's your moment when you personally embraced Jesus Christ as Savior. Some of you could tell me the exact time and place where that happened. For others that moment may be less distinct. Your personal relationship with Jesus may have developed over a long time—perhaps a month, six months, a year or longer. But at some point in your journey, you knew you were trusting in Jesus alone for your salvation and you accepted that for yourself. You knew you were forgiven. You knew beyond a shadow of a doubt that you are going to Heaven when you die. You knew you were no longer trusting in your own efforts, your own works but trusting entirely on His work for you on the Cross. If that's the case, you've had your moment!"

> *"Everyone needs to have what I call 'your moment.'"*

At that point I lifted up my Bible and opened it to the very front page. "Something you may find helpful is to write down the date of your 'moment' in the front of your Bible. For example, my moment was February of 1954, in my bedroom in State College, Pennsylvania. I was seven years old at the time, and had just asked my dad if I was really a Christian. He reminded me that I had asked Jesus to be my Savior two years before, when I was five. It bothered me that I couldn't recall the events surrounding that decision, so later that evening when everything in the house was quiet, I got out of bed, knelt by my window, looked up into the dark winter sky and prayed, 'God, if five is too young to know You, maybe seven is old enough. Please come into my heart.' That is the 'moment' I have written down in the front of my Bible."

That evening at dinner I eagerly looked for Camille and Bob so I could explain what was going to happen at Victory Circle. We always had a time of worship and singing around the campfire, followed by conferees sharing what the Lord had accomplished in their lives over the week. The culmination would be sharing the Lord's Table together. Knowing Camille and Bob approached the Lord's Table in a different manner, I wanted to be sure they would be comfortable with our particular tradition. As much as I searched, I was unable to find them before Victory Circle so I asked the Lord to give them comfort and understanding, and then I joined the guests at the campfire.

It was a wonderful evening. As the sun went down the evening air cooled, both soothing and invigorating. We heard some special testimonies of how the Lord had used speakers, worship times, quiet walks, summer staff, mealtime conversations and personal times with Him to make important differences in people's lives. After we finished with the Lord's Table, we sang a song and were dismissed to our celebration on the Commons. There were games, popcorn, cotton candy, ice cream, and animal balloons set up under the redwoods.

I meandered through the crowd, chatting with some of the new friends I had made during the week, dear friends from other years, and some of our incredible staff members who work so hard to pull off an event of this nature. I hadn't been out there very long when a man I didn't know came up to me with a young boy hanging from each arm.

"Are you Roger Williams?" he asked, looking a little uncomfortable.

"Yes I am."

"I'm Bob Franicevich. I have a message from my wife Camille, who I believe you have already met."

"I have met your wife."

"Well, she's unable to talk right now." As he spoke, he motioned over his left shoulder. I looked past him to see her standing about ten feet behind him, sobbing.

"What's wrong?" I asked.

"I'm an environmental engineer," said Bob, "so I'm not sure I understand all that's going on here—but Camille wanted me to tell you that today in your seminar she had her moment! I'm not sure what she is talking about, and I don't think it has happened to me, but do you know what that means?"

Bob & Camille Franicevich with Rachel & Roger

I smiled. "Yes, I do, Bob. That's just wonderful. And when she can talk about it more fully, I believe you'll see it the same way." I was thrilled!

"Okay," he responded. "I believe you."

I knew what I wanted to do next, but felt I better make sure I it was okay with Bob. "May I have permission to give your wife a hug?"

"Well...yes," he stammered. I guessed he probably hadn't ever been asked that question before.

I walked over to Camille, gave her a hug, and told her how happy I was that she had had her 'moment', "Actually," I added, "I was looking for you before dinner to talk to you about the Lord's Table so that you wouldn't feel uncomfortable with our tradition."

"Are you kidding?" Camille said, her face glowing, "That was the most powerful Eucharist we have ever experienced!"

"Roger," Bob interrupted, "this has been an incredible week. I mean it. As a matter of fact we have purchased tapes of every session and every speaker. I have already called my boss and asked for another week off. We're going off somewhere and listen to these messages all over again."

"That's fantastic," I replied. No one had ever said that to me before. "If you have any questions, don't hesitate to get in contact with me."

The next morning I ran into them one last time at breakfast. After a bit of small talk, Camille said, "You know Roger, we've been thinking. We'd like to have a Mount Hermon Open House at our home in Santa Rosa to let some of our friends from church and the neighborhood know about Family Camp. Would that be okay?"

"That's an awesome idea. And if it's all right with you, I'd like to be the staff person that comes to your home to do the Open House."

We stayed in touch through the fall and winter. In early spring I jumped in my Jeep Cherokee and made my way up to Santa Rosa. When I left Mount Hermon it was a gorgeous spring day with the sun shining, and not a cloud in the sky. The temperature was perfect. But as I drove closer to San Francisco, the skies turned gray, then dark. By the time I passed the city and drove north towards Santa Rosa it was raining lightly.

I arrived in Santa Rosa to a downpour. I found Bob and Camille's very comfortable home and parked. Then I discovered there was no roof protecting the front door. I really didn't want to get soaked while I knocked so I decided to sit in my car a bit longer in hopes the rain would subside.

It didn't.

It only got worse.

Finally I could wait no longer. I grabbed the boxes of information about Mount Hermon that I needed for the evening, jumped out of the car, sprinted to the front door, and knocked furiously. Bob answered.

Even before he opened the door I was soaked to the skin. But what happened next took it to a new level.

"Good evening, Bob!" I said, as enthusiastically as I could, already feeling like a drowned rat.

"Oh Roger, Roger, Roger," Bob began in a more excited tone than I had ever heard him use before. "Guess what?"

"What?"

"I'VE HAD MY MOMENT!!

Now I was as happy as he was.

"When we came home from Mount Hermon, we listened to the tapes and talked and talked and talked. Then Billy Graham came to the Bay Area for his crusade. I went forward when he gave the invitation. I'VE HAD MY MOMENT!"

The whole time he was sharing his story with excitement, I was standing in the pouring rain. Suddenly he realized my predicament.

"Oh, dear! Come in, come in, Roger!"

Camille took one look at me and laughed out loud. "Roger, we're gonna need to do something about those wet clothes."

And that's the reason I had dinner with them that night in one of Bob's bathrobes while everything I owned (and I do mean everything) was taking a much-needed spin in the clothes dryer. Camille had prepared a wonderful homemade gnocchi, and they told me about their rich family heritage.

By dinner's end, I was able to put on dry clothes, and we welcomed a house full of friends who were eager and curious to hear about Mount Hermon. Many of the couples that attended that Open House became "regulars" at our family conferences throughout the years. Thanks to the faithful ministry of Bob and Camille, people are continually being introduced to what it means to have a personal relationship with Jesus. And they've introduced many new friends to Mount Hermon. They both teach Bible studies, and their oldest son's goal is to enter the ministry. They are a wonderful example of the many whose lives have been transformed by encountering Jesus at Mount Hermon.

And it all started with their "moment."

Have you had yours?

presented to

Mt. Hermon Association by

Mr. and Mrs. Charles H. Hunt

in memory of

Dr. Lapsley McAfee

May 30 1949

CHH
5/
49.

Walnut from old senate wall
by Abraham Lincoln. Brot to California
by sailing vessel. then by team
to San Jose the State Capitol
owned by Congressman Houghton.

TWELVE

Hearing from Heaven for Over a Century

Do not be anxious about anything, but in every situation, by prayer and petition, with thanksgiving, present your requests to God.

PHILIPPIANS 4:6 (NIV)

IN 2001—OUR 95TH YEAR OF PROVIDING CHRISTIAN CAMP AND CONFERENCE PROGRAMS—THE MOUNT HERMON BOARD OF DIRECTORS TOOK UP THE ALL-IMPORTANT ISSUE FOR OUR NEXT CENTURY OF MINISTRY. The biggest question was how to keep Mount Hermon relevant and vital.

After a good deal of discussion at various levels, we reached important conclusions. No question about it. We needed to strategically add some new facilities to prepare us for the future. This would require launching a capital campaign. We decided to call it the Centennial Campaign since it was to conclude in 2006—our 100TH year of ministry on these grounds.

Ron Singley, our newly elected Chairman of the Board of Directors, brought two issues to the Board's attention. First, what should be the primary focus for the Centennial Campaign and second, what would be the campaign's scope? Initially the Board believed building a new auditorium should take priority, but when members asked our staff that question, they cast their vote for a recreation structure.

The Board felt this was a good suggestion since nearly two-thirds of our guests come in the fall, winter, and spring. Many of

PREVIOUS Inscription etched inside of the clock that had hung in the back of the chapel since 1949 those guests came during northern California's rainy season, when it's more difficult to enjoy and use the outdoor recreation facilities. At the time, tiny Forest Hall housed our only indoor recreation options—three ping-pong tables and three foosball tables. This certainly didn't provide enough recreation for guests at our large winter retreats when it was raining outside. Later, a feasibility study conducted by our fundraising consultant confirmed this need, so we made a recreational facility our main focus.

The second question was more challenging—what should be the scope? The scope of the campaign refers to how much money we'd need to raise. Ron and I had been discussing and praying about this for months. It was wonderful to have a man as the Chairman of the Board who also happened to be my mentor and dear friend. Many evenings Ron and I would sit on the deck of my home, talking and praying about Mount Hermon's future. As we prayed, we began to hear God moving us to trust Him in a huge way. He was giving us numbers in a range that would be very challenging.

Once again, God's timing was perfect. Even down to the moment a Board meeting stops for a restroom break. On September 29, 2001, the Board was conducting its regularly scheduled fall meeting. We went through several items on the agenda before talking about the campaign. Sensing we needed a break, Ron announced, "Let's take ten minutes for a break and then we'll come back to discuss the scope of the Centennial Campaign."

Like most others in the room, I made my way to the Men's Room and entered the first available stall. Several Board members followed soon after, but they had no idea I was already there. Thus, I was privy to certain conversations I otherwise would not have heard.

"What was the scope of our last campaign?" I heard one member ask another.

"That would be raising funds for the new dining hall," came the reply. "It was around $7.2 million—but it took ten years to raise it."

"The Centennial Campaign is set for four years—less than half the ten-year duration—so maybe we should look at a $3 million dollar scope," replied the other.

There was a moment with no talking and then the first board member added, "Well, that was more than ten years ago, so you have to figure in inflation. Maybe we can go for $3.5 million."

I was shocked. The number they were bantering around was certainly less than the number Ron and I had been hearing from Heaven. Significantly less. I waited until I heard the Men's Room clear out, then made my escape unnoticed. I quickly found Ron, took him aside and said, "Ron, we have some real divergence on a number here." I proceeded to tell him what I had overheard. He listened quietly. A few minutes later he called the meeting back to order.

"According to our agenda, it's time to discuss the scope of the Centennial Campaign," he began. He paused, as if he was looking for the right words to say. "I now realize this issue is far too significant to the ministry of Mount Hermon to decide casually."

I nodded and noticed others were nodding in agreement as well.

"I'd like to suggest a weekend retreat where the focus would be entirely on prayer."

"So," he continued, "I'd like to suggest a weekend retreat where the focus would be entirely on prayer—where we can ask the Lord what His will is on this matter. Rather than plunge ahead, let's hear from Heaven."

Everyone thought it was a wonderful idea—the right idea. We left that Board meeting with the assignment to work on coordinating a weekend where we could all assemble together at Mount Hermon for a weekend of prayer. We set a date for the following January. The plans for the Prayer Retreat were in motion.

Among the characteristics I've always admired about our Board are their commitment to Jesus Christ, their godliness, their love for Mount Hermon's ministry and their spiritual maturity. Many of the members of our Board of Directors are—or have been—successful business executives. They are persons of action not shying away from decisions. Consequently, I was expecting a couple of phone calls from Board members inquiring about our prayer retreat. The first one went something like this:

"Roger, I'm calling to see if you could give me a preview of the schedule for the Prayer Retreat."

"We'll begin Friday evening with dinner. Afterwards we'll pray until bedtime. Saturday morning we'll have breakfast, and then pray until lunch. After lunch we'll pray some more, share the Lord's Table together, and then be dismissed in the late afternoon."

After a hefty pause on the other end of the phone, the person asked, "How do you pray that long?"

"Trust me," I replied, "You'll find that time will be very meaningful and pass quickly. I'm guessing we'll all wish we had *more* time!"

And that's exactly what happened. The time flew as we prayed together—sometimes as a whole group—sometimes in small groups— sometimes alone so we could listen. As the retreat leader, Ron began each session with a fifteen-minute teaching time on some aspect related to our goal. I specifically remember him telling us about King David calling the leaders of Israel together and encouraging them to be models of giving. Then we would go to our knees.

At the conclusion of the retreat, Ron instructed us by saying, "We'll discuss this issue at our February Board meeting a month from now. Between now and then, just keep praying. Let's not have any discussion of this matter among ourselves until we all meet together next month. Why? Because it's not about hearing from one another—it's about hearing from Heaven."

The Board members honored Ron's request.

It was a foggy winter's day when the February meeting rolled around. There was a certain mixture of excitement and nervousness among the members. To heighten the drama, there were six or seven other action items preceding the one listed as "Scope of the Centennial Campaign." You could feel the tension increasing as we approached that last item on the agenda. The time had finally arrived.

"So what have you been hearing from Heaven?" Those were the exact words Ron used to bring up the issue. As if on cue, the moment he raised the question, everyone in the room lowered their head, staring at the table in front of them. It was clear from the body language, no one wanted to be first to speak.

Ron allowed the silence to sift around the table for what seemed like a long time. Finally, a Board member lifted his eyes and moved his head forward, like a turtle from his shell, and said in barely a whisper, "I know this sounds crazy, but I keep hearing $20 million." As soon as he said it, he quickly lowered his head.

I'm sure he thought it a shocking amount, so imagine his amazement when another Board member across from him agreed, "That's the same number I've been hearing, but I didn't have the courage to say it out loud!"

"I heard that number as well," affirmed another Board member.

"Me, too," agreed yet another.

In less than a minute, every Board member had affirmed that number!

It was a powerful moment that brought goose bumps to every person in the room.

"Well, let's make it official," Ron said. "Let's take a vote." And with that, the Mount Hermon Board of Directors unanimously approved the figure of $20 million for the goal of the Centennial Campaign. We had now agreed to start the largest capital campaign ever attempted by a single camp entity in the United States— something we were unaware of at the time.

Within a few days of that meeting, I received a phone call from a prominent Christian leader in the Bay Area. "Roger, could you possibly have picked a worse time to launch your campaign?"

I knew what he was saying. Some time later the Wall Street Journal would call this period the "First Silicon Valley Recession." Yet I knew we had heard clearly from the Lord. So I responded, "Actually I think this is the BEST time to launch this campaign. It won't be skimming the excess off huge earnings from the IPOs of the last decade, or cash from the coffers of the corporate entities in the Silicon Valley. It will only be successful if God shows up in power and makes this happen. And when that occurs, He will get all the glory, not us."

"I see." My friend seemed to be at a loss of words.

"It's not about IPOs, real estate values or 401Ks or recessions. It's the sacrificial giving of God's people. Our Board has heard from Heaven—we're an empowered bunch—we're going full steam ahead."

Now to put these numbers into perspective. Between the overheard conversation in the restroom, where the number $3.5 million was thrown around, and the $20 million we decided upon, a feasibility study had been done on our behalf and it came back with the number $12 million preferable—$14 million at the maximum. So taking on $20 million was a God-sized endeavor.

The campaign began splendidly. Menlo Park Presbyterian Church called us and asked us to make a presentation to a Foundation. It was before all our plans were cast and we had nothing printed at that point. We didn't have much time to prepare anything professional. But with our hand-printed posters and homespun methods, the Foundation agreed to give us $1 million—the largest gift we had received to that point. Shortly after that gift, there were others and pretty quickly we had $4 million raised.

All of these stories are amazing, but one best illustrates how God was at work on our behalf. During the first summer of our campaign, a couple attended our Labor Day Conference. Eric and Marguerite McAfee lived over in the Bay Area and were familiar with Mount Hermon. Eric was very successful in the venture capital world. He and his wife wandered around the grounds one afternoon when they decided to poke their heads into our lovely little Chapel. It is a wonderful spot for quiet reflection and meditation. After they spent a bit of time there, they turned to leave. As they were walking out, Marguerite noticed an antique wooden clock on the back wall. It was old and in disrepair, the most obvious malady being it no longer had hands. Underneath the clock hung a scratched plaque that read:

This clock was given in honor of Reverend L.A. McAfee, Pastor, First Presbyterian Church of Berkeley, California.

Eric and Marguerite looked at one another in disbelief. "I'm pretty sure that is your great-grandfather," Marguerite concluded. And it turned out she was correct.

As the couple did more investigating into their family's historic connection with Mount Hermon, they became increasingly excited about our Centennial Campaign, as well. Their enthusiasm caused them to feel led by God to make a significant financial gift to our endeavor—$2 million dollars!

I was searching for a meaningful way to express appreciation to this dear couple on behalf of Mount Hermon, when an idea came to me. Why not

The restored clock that now hangs in the McAfee's home

present them with the clock they had seen hanging in the back of the Chapel to place in their home until we could create a place to display it when the new auditorium was completed? We could have it restored so it would actually run. I checked with one of our staff, asking him to meet me over at the Chapel so we could take the clock off the wall to see what restoration might be in order.

As the two of us carefully handled the clock, we observed there was a hand-lettered inscription on the inside back of the clock. The words I read shocked me:

Presented to Mount Hermon Association by
Mr. and Mrs. Charles H. Hunt
In memory of
Dr. Lapsley McAfee

May 30, 1949

Walnut from old wardrobe used
By Abraham Lincoln. Brot to San Francisco
By sailing vessel then by stage
To San Jose the State Capital
Owned by Senator Houghton

We ended up doing some research and discovered that the beautiful walnut from which this clock was hand-made did indeed come from a wardrobe that belonged to Abraham Lincoln. After his death, the clock, along with other pieces of Lincoln's furniture, were sent by ship from Washington, D.C. to our own Bay Area. There was no Panama Canal in those days, so the voyage required the ship to sail around the bottom of South America on its way back up the West Coast of the Americas. Apparently the seas were stormy and much of the furniture on board was severely damaged due to the violent movements of the ship.

When the wardrobe was carried off the ship, it was in poor condition but Senator Houghton later repaired it. Years after that, it was torn apart—nothing left but a pile of beautiful antique walnut. At this point the man who built this clock, a woodworker, used the wood to build a clock as a way to honor his faithful pastor.

Today the timepiece is fully restored and hangs proudly in the home of Eric and Marguerite McAfee. In many ways, it is a testament to God's faithfulness, seen in the life of a faithful pastor, who would so impact a member of his congregation that the man would offer him this gift of love and honor, to the glory of God. In the same way, the generous financial gift from his great-grandson and wife demonstrates the same thing—a gift of love and honor to the glory of God.

But the story of the Centennial Campaign is far from completed. God had much more in store—further miraculous events to move us toward the financial goal our Board had unanimously heard from Heaven that wintry February day.

THIRTEEN

A Tutorial from Heaven... An Intriguing Email

You are the God who performs miracles;

you display your power among the peoples.

PSALMS 77:14 (NIV)

R AISING $20 MILLION IS NO SMALL ASSIGNMENT, YET WE HAD TREMENDOUS PEACE THIS WAS GOD'S NUMBER FOR MOUNT HERMON IN OUR CENTENNIAL CAMPAIGN.

At the outset of the campaign, the Board knew this was uncharted territory for many of us, so they suggested we bring in a fundraising consultant who could help us learn the most effective ways to conduct a campaign of this magnitude.

The consultant's donor fundraising strategy was fairly simple: begin by isolating our donors into one of three categories. Those who had the potential to give gifts of $1 million or more were referred to as *Lead Donors*. Those who could give $100,000 or more were called *Major Donors* and the rest would be *Donors*. Obviously, those three categories fell into the shape of a triangle, or pyramid.

Once the donors were categorized, the next step was, in the words of our consultant: "Do background research on your lead and major donors, meet with them and then ask them for *double* what you think they can give."

"Double?" I inquired.

PREVIOUS Centennial Campaign Gala

"Don't worry, Roger," he assured me. "That amount will honor them. They will be flattered you think they can give that much." He smiled and added, "As you articulate that amount, you may receive a gift even larger than they originally planned."

I had been raising money for years in my work directing Christian camps and conference centers, but I had never been involved in a "formal" capital campaign. So, based of my lack of experience coupled with my respect for our Board and their consultant, I agreed with the plan. I was to conduct our first donor appointment. Little did I know how significant it would be.

Our consultant had set up a breakfast meeting with a couple he knew to be interested in Mount Hermon. "Go see them, Rog," he advised. "Share the contents of the campaign, and then I want you to ask them for a *half million dollars!*"

From my business days selling computers, I had experience in presenting proposals of this size (and larger). This task didn't seem all that daunting, and I was much more excited about the ministry dimensions of Mount Hermon than gigabytes of storage or RAM memory. We met at a hotel restaurant in Scotts Valley. I enjoyed chatting with this lovely couple about a variety of topics, including our ministry. When the time seemed appropriate, I presented the campaign specifics and did what I was told to do.

"I'd like you to consider giving Mount Hermon $500,000 for this campaign."

It got real quiet as normally happens. I was trained to let it stay silent until they spoke next.

"We will talk about it and get back to you." The reply struck me as cautious, though polite.

I thanked them for their time and the breakfast ended.

I paid the bill, walked out of the restaurant, got in my car, and the tutorial began, God's tutorial—a tutorial from Heaven.

So you've just had your first meeting for the Centennial Campaign and now—after all these years—you've figured out a new way to provide for Mount Hermon.

"No Lord," I replied, "we're still trusting in You." No question this was the Lord speaking and He definitely had something He wanted me to hear. I started the car and drove out of the parking lot.

Roger, how have I met Mount Hermon's needs in the past? How have I protected and provided for Mount Hermon for nearly a century?

I stammered out a few responses and finally hit the one the Lord wanted me to express, "People prayed, went forward in the dark, and trusted you to provide," I replied.

Right, He said. *And now it's research, "ask for double and hope they give you more than planned"* the Lord pressed on.

"Yes, You're right," I admitted.

And just what motive appeal are you addressing with this "doubling notion?"

I didn't want to answer that question, but I had no choice. This was a direct conversation with the Lord of the Universe. "Well, Lord," I answered, "they are supposed to feel flattered, so I guess the basic motive appeal is pride."

That's right. Thanks for your honesty.

"I'm getting the message loud and clear, Lord. You want us to change this process. What do you want us to do—what is your desired strategy for Mount Hermon to use as we share the campaign with donors?"

Share the vision of the campaign. Share it compellingly. Share the results of transformed lives. Then, ask them to pray about what I would have them do. Assure them they need to hear from Heaven before they ever give one dollar to Mount Hermon. I may want them to invest their dollars in another of my Kingdom ministries. And when they do hear from Heaven, then encourage them to be obedient to what they hear.

Also, let them know that their relationship with Mount Hermon won't be affected by whether they give or not. That's how I want you to do it.

"Thank You, Lord," I whispered. "I've got it." With that, I parked my car back at Mount Hermon and headed for the office to place a call to our consultant. He wanted a first-hand report.

"How did your breakfast meeting go?" he asked with excitement in his voice.

"It went fine."

"Did you ask them for the half million dollars?"

"Yes, I surely did."

"You did?" He actually sounded surprised that I had done what I was told to do. "This is good, a great start. This is how the campaign will be successful. We'll be doing lots more of this."

Before he could go any further in expressing his enthusiasm, I interrupted him. "I need to tell you something. This is the last time I'm going to do this."

There was a very long pause on the other end of the phone. "What do you mean by that?"

"This is the last time I'm ever going to ask someone for a specific sum of money for this campaign," I replied.

"But Roger, this is how major donor fundraising works," he argued.

"Not at Mount Hermon."

"Well, what do you propose?" He sounded incredulous.

I told him exactly what the Lord had said to me in my tutorial during the drive back from the hotel.

"Roger, I've been in this business for thirty years and I can tell you that approach will never work."

"Never?"

"Never!"

After another period of silence I spoke. "Let me ask you a question. Do you believe the Lord has unlimited resources at His beck and call?"

"Yes, of course."

"Second question. Do you believe God can communicate to His children how He wants those resources to be invested?"

"Yes," he slowly agreed.

"This is what I am proposing as our strategy," I stated. "I want the Lord to direct this campaign in every regard so that when it concludes, He—and He alone—will get the glory. It won't be us with our incisive research and strategic tasks."

> *"I want the Lord to direct this campaign in every regard so that when it concludes, He—and He alone—will get the glory."*

After a pause he added, "You sound very confident in what you're proposing, Roger. What happened?"

"I'm fresh out of a personal tutorial with the Lord. You remember Balaam? Well, my vehicle became a donkey on the way back from the hotel. I'm sharing with you the results of that divine encounter."

"I'm telling you it won't work," he pronounced. "And remember, it's your neck!"

"No," I replied. "It's not my neck because this is not my ministry. Mount Hermon doesn't belong to me or the Board. It belongs to the Lord, and I'm convinced we need to follow His direction."

At this point in the story I should add some important follow-up information concerning the integrity of our fundraising consultant. About a year after this phone conversation, he came back to me and said, "Roger, I am grateful that you stuck to your guns on this issue. It's joyful for me to watch how God is providing for Mount Hermon." Another year passed and he shared with me he was now teaching major donor fundraising differently as a result of the Mount Hermon experience.

As a consequence of God's tutorial, I can honestly say that *no donor to our Centennial Campaign was ever asked for a specific amount of money.* The couple I met for breakfast that morning never gave us any money for our campaign, so they can't be considered donors. I wondered whether we had lost them as friends of the ministry so I am delighted to say that the woman (by that time a widow) ended up on a Mount Hermon cruise a few years later, allowing me the opportunity to apologize for any offense my behavior might have caused that morning at the hotel restaurant. She had been offended, and graciously accepted my apology. Then, she was thrilled to hear how that appointment had been the starting point in providing the new strategy for the rest of the campaign.

• • •

In the fall of 2003, we launched a series of big banquets in order to present the vision of the Centennial Campaign to interested constituents and friends. We wanted them to hear about our vision so they could pray about their involvement with us.

The banquets were quite an undertaking, since our goal was to reproduce Mount Hermon in a hotel banquet room. As people entered the room, the sounds of birds singing and chirping, and wind in tall trees, greeted them, thanks to an audiotape playing over the sound system. These nature sounds had been recorded at Mount Hermon deep in our Bean Creek canyon. Each table had a small redwood tree as a centerpiece, symbolizing the mighty trees that were so much a part of our landscape. The stage was constructed to look like Mount Hermon as well, with lots of small Redwood trees and a few large tree trunks made out of Redwood bark. The Lord used those banquets to make thousands of people aware of our vision and needs.

In the fall of 2004, Ron Singley's tenure as Chairman of the Board concluded. He passed the torch to the able Rob Faisant. The Centennial Campaign was moving right along, but as we approached 2005, we seemed stuck at approximately $14.5 million, $5.5 short of our $20 million dollar goal.

We had plateaued. We remained at $14.5 million for over six months, with virtually no movement. Right before the December board meeting, Rob pulled me aside and candidly asked, "Roger, can you think of anything we can do at this point?"

"No," I replied. "We're just waiting on the Lord. We've shared the vision of the campaign with everyone we know. From my perspective, we are doing all that we know to do."

Rob pondered my answer. "What if we scheduled another Prayer Retreat?"

"Great idea!"

So, as Ron Singley had done before him, Rob Faisant asked all the Board members at our December meeting to check their calendars. We agreed on Friday, February 18, 2005 for the day of our next Board Prayer Retreat.

We assembled the night before, Thursday, February 17TH and spent the evening in praise and thanksgiving for all the Lord had done—and was doing—at Mount Hermon. We were very specific in our expressions of gratitude, and it encouraged us all to remember God's faithfulness in answering prayer in the past few months. We had decided to not only pray, but also fast all day Friday the 18TH, breaking the fast with dinner that evening. Friday morning at eight o'clock, we began with a devotional on the purpose of fasting and then began our prayer time on our knees.

But to fully understand the significance of what happened on that day, I need to backtrack a bit. Two months, actually.

Five days after our December Board meeting, on December 15, 2004, I had received an email. It read:

An overseas donor wishes to make a contribution toward your project. Please send us your bank name and bank account number.

It was signed by a member of a chartered accountancy firm located in London. I checked the company website and discovered the signer was not one of the principles in the organization. At this point, conventional wisdom would say this was a scam, it was bogus, so beware. But for some reason I can't explain, I did not hit the delete button. I printed it out and prayed about it at my desk. I tried to throw the paper away twice, but each time I felt the Holy Spirit stopping me, and I'd return it to my desk.

After a couple of hours, and several rounds of prayer, I decided to take a stroll in the late afternoon down the hall to the accounting department, specifically to see my friends and co-workers, Alden Johanson and Scott Halverson. I let them read the email.

"You're going to throw this away, right?" they said at once as they read the email text. "This is just another scam, like the Prince from the African nation that is making millions available to you if you give him all your banking information."

> *"What if this is God's way of surprising us, doing something beyond our expectations, and being strong on our behalf?"*

For some reason I couldn't see it that way. "No, I'm not throwing it away at this point," I replied. "I'm going to take it home tonight, and pray about it."

They looked at me as though I'd lost it!

"What if this is God's way of surprising us, doing something beyond our expectations, and being strong on our behalf?" I asked.

Both Alden and Scott rolled their eyes in disbelief, but to their credit, they didn't attempt to override me.

I went home that night and prayed earnestly for God to show me what to do. But by the next day, the only clear message I had was to hold onto it.

The following morning the guys asked me if I gotten rid of the email.

"No," I replied, still feeling like this might be something God was doing. "What if we set up a separate bank account exclusively for this potential donor? It should be a deposit-only account with just one person cleared to access it. That way the firm's representative wouldn't have any information that would allow him to remove any funds from Mount Hermon, right? How long would that take?" I asked.

"About twenty minutes."

"That's what I'd like you to do," I said.

The guys reluctantly agreed it was a strategy that wouldn't cause any Mount Hermon funds to be in danger, so they agreed to do what I requested (albeit a little grudgingly)!

Later that day, I hit the reply button and emailed back our bank name and a new bank account number to the people in London. I received an immediate reply that said they appreciated our attention to this matter and we'd be hearing from them in a couple of weeks before the end of the year.

Well, many weeks passed with no word from anyone in London. Christmas came and went, and it was now the end of January. Be assured, I was taking a fair amount of kidding from the guys who knew what was going on. All I could do was respond, "Are you praying about this?" They would just smile and walk away.

It was beginning to look like the accounting guys were right. Perhaps this was nothing more than a scam. Even my secretary at the time, Priscilla Weiss, took it upon herself to write a personal email to our contact in London expressing her disappointment if this was a joke, because it was making her boss, the Director, look bad. (I didn't know she had done this, but when I heard I was grateful for her support.)

Early in February we received a reply stating they were sorry for the long delay—key people were on holiday, signatures taking longer to obtain—and asking us to remain patient, it would all be coming together shortly. In this response to Priscilla's email they said we should be hearing from the bank very soon.

The day before the Board Prayer Retreat Thursday, February 17TH, I received an email with a bank logo and two sentences on it:

> *Thank you for letting us be of service to you. The transaction has been completed into your account.*

It arrived at 4:50 p.m. while I was on the phone. At about 5:15 p.m. I noticed it on my computer and got excited.

I walked down the hall to the accounting department to show the guys what I had received. "Anyone can send something like this. Anyone can copy that logo. There isn't even a name on the email." Their responses were understandably skeptical.

"Can we call the bank and check on this?" I asked.

"Not today. The bank is already closed. We can call tomorrow after nine.

"Well, you and I will be on our knees praying with the Board at the Board Prayer Retreat," I replied. "So if one of your staff will call tomorrow and bring a note to me regarding the balance in that special account, I will appreciate it."

The next morning, Friday February 18TH, the Board members and the executive staff began to pray. At around 9:40 a.m., a staff member found me and handed me a slip of paper, but since I was praying I placed it in my pocket and continued.

At 10:00 a.m. we stopped our prayer time to take a short break. It was at that moment that I reached into my pocket to see what the message contained. Before we were dismissed, I raised my hand in order to get Rob Faisant's attention. He acknowledged me.

"Mr. Chairman," I began, "I know that some of us need to use the restroom, but I have a question—what have we just been praying for? The Board members began to respond, "We've run out of our own ideas, and we've been praying for God to show us His power." "We need Him to provide resources for our campaign." "We need His help to move forward." "We need Him to be strong on our behalf." Everyone agreed this was our prayer focus, but found it strange I was asking this question when everyone was ready for a break.

"Gentleman and ladies," I continued, "last night just before 5:00 p.m., $1,089,504.70 was deposited into our campaign account— and I have absolutely no idea where it came from!"

There was a hush throughout the entire room. We were in utter shock. This was like praying for Peter's release from prison when Peter showed up. We were asking God to do something to help us, and He did it in an amazing and big way. Finally a Board member found his voice and broke the silence by saying very slowly, "We... need...to...thank...the...Lord! We...need...to...praise...Him!"

It was one of the greatest moments I have ever experienced. We started thanking Him, praising Him, exalting Him. We were singing and praying all at once! He did what we could not do.

That gift re-ignited the campaign. By late fall of 2005 we had reached the campaign goal in slightly less than three years—more than one full year ahead of schedule. The Lord had provided $20 million. What was the key? *Prayer.*

We had heard from Heaven, by way of a personal tutorial that moved prayer right back into the center of our campaign process. We had heard from Heaven by means of an odd foreign email that was only responded to because of prayer. The old adage is still true. Our inscrutable God often works in mysterious ways His wonders to perform.

FOURTEEN

Blessings Above & Beyond

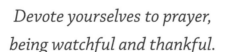

Devote yourselves to prayer,
being watchful and thankful.

COLOSSIANS 4:2 (NIV)

WHEN THE BOARD APPROVED $20 MILLION AS THE GOAL FOR OUR CENTENNIAL CAMPAIGN, IT WAS ABOUT $6 MILLION ABOVE THE MAXIMUM LEVEL OUR CONSULTANT HAD PROJECTED WE COULD EXPECT. We were "trusting big." It was a God-sized goal. Ironically, however, it was a smaller number than Ron Singley and I heard from Heaven back when we first started praying over these issues long before the Campaign was launched.

The two of us were hearing more along the lines of $30–40 million.

"Why would God put that number on our hearts, when the Board unanimously agreed on $20 million?" we asked ourselves. We had no answer to that question, and the campaign was launched.

But God was at work.

During the second year of the campaign, our Outdoor Science School Director, Dr. Rick Oliver, came by my office, exclaiming to my administrative assistant, Priscilla, "I have to see Roger!"

"What's up, Rick? You seem pretty excited," I began, as we sat around the table in my office.

PREVIOUS Horse pasture at Kidder Creek

"Rog, Susan (Rick's wife) and I met this couple in a parking lot—Harry and Nancy Batrum—and we began having this discussion about creation versus evolution. It started casually enough, but then it turned serious and substantive. Before I knew it, they invited us to their house for lunch. So we drove to their home and the conversation continued."

"Okay." I nodded, still not sure where this conversation was going and how it included me. "Go on."

"After lunch they told me they're on the Board of a camp called 'Dry Bones.' It's about eighteen miles inland from the Hearst Castle in California. The history of this land goes all the way back to a Spanish Land Grant. The great-great grandson of the original owner bought a hundred and sixty acres to create a camp on part of that property. Today, a local pastor and Harry and Nancy Batrum are the three Board members. The camp is still only partially developed and currently they have no full-time staff."

He paused and leaned forward, lowered his voice telegraphing that what he was about to say was important. And it was.

"Rog, they want to know *if Mount Hermon would be interested in this camp?*"

I sat quietly for a moment, trying to take it all in. "What do you think they mean by 'being interested' in their camp?"

"I honestly don't know. Perhaps they want us to take it over. However I'm not sure what they're talking about."

"Let me run this by our Board Chairman, Ron Singley," I decided. "We'll see what he thinks." I have to admit I had a premonition that God was about to do something unexpected and exciting.

Rick agreed it was a good strategy and left my office. I immediately got hold of Ron, who was also my neighbor, and told him about the conversation with Rick. "Can you come up to my house? We need to start with prayer," Ron replied and that's exactly what we did. After praying for a while, we felt a freedom from the

Lord and the next day I contacted Harry and Nancy, arranging for a time to visit with them and tour the camp.

About a week later, we drove south to visit the Batrums. We immediately hit it off with them, greatly enjoying this new friendship. They freely volunteered to us that other larger camps had been nibbling at the possibility of taking over the camp, but because they knew Mount Hermon and its reputation, and because they so respected the passion for Biblical truth displayed in the conversation with Dr. Oliver, they became increasingly comfortable with the possibility of us taking over their camp.

Eventually I had to ask the difficult and clarifying question. "In your thinking, how would this arrangement play out?"

Their answer floored me.

"If you were interested in taking us over, we'd like to give the camp to you."

Ron and I were stunned. This was a beautiful property nestled between Lake San Antonio and Lake Nacimiento. Thirty of the one hundred sixty acres were relatively flat, allowing development of multiple camp structures and recreation zones. The remaining

Whisper Canyon

acreage was a beautiful deep canyon where the floor of the valley harbored a small stream and huge old valley oak trees, complete with rock walls. Ron and I were very excited about adding this site to our family of camps. Given its location, we began our initial plans envisioning a water sports camp for this property since it was only a short distance to either Lake San Antonio or Lake Nacimiento. Did we have any boats—powerboats, sailboats, kayaks, etc? No! Mount Hermon's existing campus was landlocked with a tiny dam on one of our creeks where you could canoe a short distance upstream. Equipment for a big lake? Nothing. Nada. That is until the year before!

When it happened, we weren't exactly sure why. But God started answering our need a year before we even knew to pray about it!

Back in late 2002, I was attending the national convention for our Christian camping association, now called the Christian Camp and Conference Association (known by the moniker CCCA). On the last day of the convention that year, they included a major prize giveaway at the closing breakfast session. The Grand Prize was a Correct Craft Competition Ski Boat, complete with trailer. The winning ticket was drawn and whom should the ticket belong to but Mount Hermon's own Fred Miller!

What happened next is comical. As soon as Fred won the boat, a line of people began developing around Fred. Why? They all knew Mount Hermon had no lake so they were hoping to purchase the boat from us. We quickly agreed not to sell the boat, at least until we got back to Mount Hermon in order to discuss our options. Once again, it was Ron Singley's response when hearing the story that directed our actions. He stated, "Let's not sell it. God gave us this boat. Let's see why."

In order to underscore what the Lord had in mind, He caused a similar circumstance to occur at the national convention the following year. I had been attempting to link up with a fellow camp director throughout the entire convention, but to no avail. We finally settled on the last possible time to meet—over breakfast at the closing session.

Just as it was done the year before, Correct Craft was once again giving away one of its Competition Ski Boats and trailers to the Grand Prize winner. To my surprise, when the winner's name was drawn, it was none other than the fellow director with whom I was seated. Immediately upon receiving the prize, he turned to me and said, "We don't have a lake. Roger. Would you like this boat?"

"Yes!" I shouted. (I know, we didn't have a lake either, but I was convinced God was up to something!)

It's a good thing I answered so quickly because, once again, other folks who directed camps with water sports programs formed an immediate line.

When I returned from the convention and shared the second boat story with Ron, he commented that he felt like Noah, who was building an ark long before the storm came. "What are you going to do with those boats?" people would ask. All we could do was smile, shrug our shoulders, and continue to watch God work.

So in 2003, after much prayer and careful study by our Board and executive team, we accepted the gift of the property known as Dry Bones with one caveat—we had to change the name. While it was originally named in commemoration of the valley of dry bones that God brought to life in the book of Ezekiel—hoping the same would happen to campers who came to this facility—it really was a tough concept to market in the twenty-first century without a lot of explanation. Our new camp name came from one of our staff, Bill Fernald, after visiting the property. While hiking around the grounds, Bill was heard to say, "Down in the canyon, it's so quiet—all the sounds of earth go away—it feels like you could hear God whisper!"

We renamed the camp "Whisper Canyon."

Today, the vision for Whisper Canyon has changed from the water sports camp we originally conceived. The Lord altered our plans as we dedicated hours of special prayer regarding its best and highest use. As we heard from Heaven, He directed us to design a facility that would better minister to the local area and would serve smaller churches that are characteristic of a large portion of central California. In short, we wanted to reach out to our "Jerusalem and Judea" in that part of the State versus "Samaria and the uttermost parts of the earth."

Today, we are working on adding new lodging facilities, an upgraded kitchen and new recreation options at Whisper Canyon. Most of this work is being accomplished by volunteers. We see its role in our family of camps as a user-friendly and beautiful site where smaller church and other faith-based ministries implement their own retreats and conferences. Our plan is to keep costs as reasonable as possible so that access to this facility is available to all who want to meet the Lord in life-changing and life-refreshing ways.

• • •

Receiving a camp as a gift was certainly above and beyond what we could ever ask or imagine. It was the first time this had ever happened in my then twenty-two years of directing Christian camps. And all this took place while the Lord was blessing our capital campaign. How could we possibly do better?

How about TWO camps?

Approximately a week before our Board would vote on the offer to accept the Whisper Canyon property, I received a phone call from Pete Morrill, who was the Executive Director of Kidder Creek Orchard Camps. Pete and I had known one another for well over ten years—most notably by both serving on the leadership planning committee of the Northern California section of CCCA. Over the last six years he had invited me up to Kidder Creek to serve as a consultant to their Board. While making those annual trips to consult, I grew to really appreciate the ministry and recreational opportunities available to their camp because of its location. I fell in love with the beauty of that part of California and naturally began developing relationships with folks in the Scott Valley, where the camp is located. Further enhancing those relationships, I had the privilege of speaking at their annual fundraising banquets several years in a row.

"Roger, I need to talk to you about a very serious matter." Pete began the phone call with a somber tone.

"How can I be of help?" I asked.

"Well, first of all, you need to listen to me for about 45 minutes without interrupting or saying a word," he continued. "Can you agree to that?"

He had become a close friend, so I cracked a big smile. "That's a severe discipline for me, as you well know, but I'll give it my best shot!"

And with that, Pete laid out a story I had not known about—not even an inkling —previous to this phone conversation. It turned out that for the last several years, Pete had been asking his Board to partner with a larger organization in order to gain greater exposure, greater excellence, greater experience and better equipping—thus helping Kidder Creek to become more effective in ministry. Mount Hermon was the larger organization Pete had in mind. He had never even hinted about this in our many times together.

But the Board of Kidder Creek was adamantly opposed to this option. They were proud of what they had accomplished over the years. They had worked hard, prayed hard, and sacrificed a lot to create and maintain this camp. And they were excited about its ministry and potential. They stayed firm in their position—until just recently.

Campers at Kidder Creek rafting down the Kalamath River

"After years of telling me not to consider this, the Board began bringing it up to me!" Pete said in surprise. "As a matter of fact, Roger, the Board has instructed me to contact you in order to see if there would be any interest on Mount Hermon's part."

My jaw had completely dropped. This idea regarding Kidder Creek had never crossed my mind. Before long, Pete had finished his 45 minutes and ended by saying, "So, what's your response?"

"First of all, I am in total shock right now," I confessed. "Secondly, the timing is very interesting, Pete. Our next Board meeting is this weekend and I will take them the offer from Whisper Canyon. Frankly, if I were to bring up Kidder Creek at the same time, I believe they would feel overwhelmed. Plus, we need time to make sure we could be good stewards of this wonderful offer. So I guess what I'm saying is that I need more time—time to pray, to consult, and to discuss this opportunity with other people I trust.

"Okay," Pete replied.

"I know what you have at Kidder," I went on. "The adventure programs you offer would really complement our Mount Hermon youth programs. With your whitewater rafting, rock climbing, wilderness programs and full horse program, this could be an incredible opportunity for all of us. I'll get back to you after our Board meeting this weekend.

"Thanks for listening and considering this, Roger," Pete replied. "And I'll trust you not to spread the word too publicly until we can both process this further." We hung up promising to stay connected.

That weekend, our Board accepted the gift of Whisper Canyon. It was a momentous day. We now had three campsites—Redwood, Ponderosa, and Whisper Canyon—in addition to the Conference Center. Once the Board meeting was over, I began telling some of the staff about Kidder Creek, so that we could pray and properly evaluate this offer. I also informed our Board Chairman, Ron Singley. He had accompanied me the last two years to help with the teaching at their Board retreats. He was very excited, but we agreed to pray quietly while our staff researched and evaluated this offer. Our staff quietly—but thoroughly—studied it for ten months to see if this would be a wise expansion proposal to bring before our Board. The more we talked with the leadership at Kidder Creek, the more the trust grew.

Initially there was discussion that Mount Hermon would be asked to clear all the indebtedness and set aside funds for an endowment to help Siskiyou County children to attend camp. But the more we communicated and prayed together, the less important the dollars became. Their Board ultimately concluded if they could trust the camp ministry to us, they could certainly trust the finances to us. Without us ever asking them to change their financial thinking, the Lord changed their hearts. They eventually offered the camp to us as an outright gift.

One of the key issues that needed to be addressed, however, was broaching this entire subject with Dick Jones, the founder of Kidder Creek Orchard Camps. He lived on the camp property and was a significant opinion leader with many of the constituents and donors in the northern California area. Their Board feared he would not be in favor of partnering with Mount Hermon, or anybody. Obviously, if he opposed it, the outcome would be very complicated indeed.

We decided that while all of us who were aware of the situation at Mount Hermon would be praying, Pete and Pam Malmberg (their current Board President) would approach Dick about this idea. As Pete and Pam started their presentation, they were apprehensive since they were unable to read Dick's body language. They couldn't tell whether he was in favor of what he was hearing or not.

About two-thirds of the way through their presentation, Dick held up his hand to interrupt them. "If you had come to me about any camping entity in California *other than Mount Hermon*, I would be opposed."

Pete and Pam's eyes widened.

Dick continued. "Back when my wife and I founded this camp, I reached out for help. I needed an advisor, a mentor, someone more experienced who could help me. I reached out to Bill Gwinn, Mount Hermon's Executive Director at the time. He came alongside to give me guidance, counsel, and encouragement as we began. There are Mount Hermon fingerprints all over this camp."

None of us knew about this.

As soon as that appointment ended, Pete called me with the good news. "Roger, God has been preparing Dick's heart all these years. He said he would enthusiastically support us in any way he can."

As I listened to the story of that meeting, I realized once again the Lord had gone before us and answered prayer.

Once Kidder's Board received Dick's blessing, we moved forward to shape the proposal we would present to our Board of Directors. It was the May 2004 Board meeting where we decided to make our presentation about Kidder Creek. On our Board, only Ron Singley had been aware of this opportunity, so with his blessing, we invited the Board members from Kidder Creek Camp to join us at the appropriate time in our Board meeting.

We worked through the agenda until we finally came to the item listed as "A New Ministry Opportunity." I stood up, cleared my throat, and began by saying, "The Lord has provided a new ministry opportunity for us to consider. I am going to ask our staff to present their findings. Our Board Chairman has also invited the Board of this ministry to be present with us today, so I'm going to invite them in at this time. The Kidder Creek Board came in and sat with our Board as our Executive Staff presented the proposal with research and rationale. "In our view, it is very strategic for Mount Hermon to acquire this property as a new camp in our family of camps," one of our staff summarized.

"Something we've held on to so tightly, we now offer to you with open hands."

After about an hour of presentation, one of our Board members turned to the Kidder Creek Board and uttered in true bewilderment, "Help me understand. You are a healthy camp with strong attendance, a dedicated staff, and a positive financial posture. Why would you want to give this to us? Why would you want to give it up?"

That is when the Holy Moment began.

One by one, each of their Board members spoke. They loved Kidder Creek. There were Board members there who had taken second mortgages on their homes in the early years to help build the camp. They'd taken their summers off work to cook in Kidder's kitchen. They spoke of the spiritual impact that camp had on the

Scott Valley, on their own children. Half of them were talking through tears as they poignantly demonstrated their deep love for their camp. One Board member put it best: "We love Kidder Creek so much, we believe by giving it away it will be a much more effective part of God's Kingdom. It will be more widely used. Mount Hermon can help it progress in five to ten years what would take us thirty or more years to accomplish. By giving it away, it will become a better, stronger camp and more powerful ministry."

"Something we've held on to so tightly, we now offer to you with open hands."

There was a complete hush in the room. Somehow in that silence, words were inadequate. Now there were tears from the people on all sides of the table. The room was "thick" with the palpable presence of the Holy Spirit. It was a God-ordained moment. Of the many hundreds of Board meetings I've attended, it was the holiest moment I have ever experienced in that setting.

Finally after a long hushed silence broken only by weeping, our Board Chairman, Ron Singley, sensitively handled the moment. "We need to pray," he whispered. And we did. Members of both Boards joined together to come boldly into God's presence. We thanked Him for the unselfishness and generosity of the Kidder Creek Board. We asked the Lord to help us be the best stewards possible of this facility, we asked Him to bless this ministry partnership, we asked Him to make this property a place where many would meet the Savior and many more be nudged closer to Him, and we asked Him to be the Lord of all at Kidder.

Then we worshiped. We savored His presence. We reveled in the quiet spaces between prayers where we communed with God. It was a holy moment indeed.

When the prayer time ended, our Board decided unanimously to accept Kidder Creek into the Mount Hermon family. It was glorious.

After the goal of the Centennial Campaign had been reached, Ron Singley and I got together to reflect on what had taken place. The Lord had provided $20 million and in the process brought us two camping properties as gifts. For the fun of it, we tried to figure out what those two properties—with their land, buildings and equipment—were worth in dollars and cents. We came up with a figure of between $10–20 million.

If you add that figure to the $20 million we raised in the Centennial Campaign, you get the figure that Ron and I had heard from Heaven before we ever began the adventure of our capital campaign—$30–$40 million.

It is a big number.

But our God is even bigger!

FIFTEEN

Prayers of Many Kinds

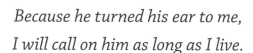

Because he turned his ear to me,
I will call on him as long as I live.

PSALMS 116:2 (NIV)

PART OF THE BEAUTY OF THE MINISTRY OF MOUNT HERMON OVER THE YEARS IS THAT PRAYER HAS BEEN SUCH A CONSISTENT AND VITAL ELEMENT. It's been at the heart of every matter for over one hundred years. And we will continue that pattern in the future.

Our Board of Directors still holds an annual Day of Prayer, which is now opened to include those special friends of Mount Hermon that are known as Associates. Usually held in May on the Friday before Mother's Day, the Board and Associates assemble for an entire day set aside to worship and praise the Lord for Who He is and then petition Him about specific Mount Hermon-related concerns.

Another prayer activity takes place in June of each year. Held on the Saturday before our camps and conference center open up for the summer programs, the Board prays for each department and group in particular. Board members visit the entire ministry, praying with the summer staff of Redwood Camp at Redwood, the summer staff of Ponderosa Lodge at Ponderosa, and the Family Camp staff at Conference Center, until all the sites of ministry have been bathed in prayer for the busy summer ministry that

PREVIOUS Great-grandma praying with her great-granddaughter at Family Camp lies ahead. (Sometimes we are able to pray with the Kidder Creek staff by teleconference!) All these locales are places for potential life transformation.

At the staff level, we have set aside every other Wednesday for an early morning prayer meeting. It is one of the highlights of the work schedule for all who are involved.

During the administration of my predecessor, Ed Hayes, a monthly Prayer Guide was established, providing a specific prayer request for each day of the month. We have kept that Prayer Guide alive ever since, now for two months at a time, instead of just one. There are over 4,000 people praying for Mount Hermon on a daily basis!

Here are a few examples of what each day might look like, taken from our actual Prayer Guide for September 2011:

SEPTEMBER 25TH
Pray for Dave Burns, Director of Adult Ministries as he effectively prepares programs to serve the needs of our guests.

SEPTEMBER 26TH
Thank the Lord for the registration staff members. They are already busy processing preregistration requests for next summer. Have you registered yet?

SEPTEMBER 27TH
Our prayer partners are crucial to the effective ministry of Mount Hermon. Thank you for your fervent prayers for Mount Hermon's staff and ministries.

We also include at the bottom of each Prayer Guide the names of three or four specific staff members to pray for each month. We are so pleased to have several thousand people as prayer partners in this ministry.

Prayer is a common thread in the fabric of life around here. Dave Talbott, who has served at Mount Hermon for over thirty years, threw his head back and laughed heartily when asked if he can remember a time where prayer at Mount Hermon was vital.

"It's always vital," he responded, "but when you asked the question, the first incident that came to mind was the night back in the late 1980s when a well-known female vocalist was booked to sing a concert here at Mount Hermon and, let's just say, it was a bit of an adventure making it come to pass.

"She was flying in from the East Coast, and even with her flight arriving on time, we knew this was going to be a close one. Ed Hayes was Executive Director at the time and he graciously volunteered to meet her at the airport and transport her safely to Mount Hermon, in time to sing.

"Well, her flight was supposed to arrive at San Francisco International Airport at 6 p.m. in order for her to sing at 8 p.m. When Ed arrived at the airport, he discovered the flight was going to be forty-five minutes late. That was going to call for a speedy drive to Mount Hermon.

"The good news is that when the singer walked off the jet way, she was already dressed in her beautiful gown. The bad news was she was coughing like she was near death's door.

"'I've been sick,' she volunteered to Ed, 'but I'll be okay—don't worry about me.'

"While we were all praying at Mount Hermon that she and Ed would make it back on time, I was beseeching God, since I was to be her accompanist, and we were not going to have time to rehearse before the concert.

"In a miracle that defies both explanation and California speed laws, Ed pulled up shortly after 8 p.m. with our soloist. She coughed and handed me a stack of music that looked as thick as a New York City phonebook and said to me, 'You'll do just fine, Dave.' And then she coughed some more.

"It was a pretty memorable concert," Dave reflects. "Our soloist would sing a song, and then cough profusely while the audience applauded. 'Please pray for me that I can make it through,' she asked the crowd. Then she sang another song, coughed and once again asked for prayer. It went on this way through the entire concert. It's the best example of a concert 'bathed in prayer' that I could have ever imagined."

———— • • • ————

Most of our stories in this book have centered upon the prayers of our leaders throughout our history. From our founders, to the Boards, to the Executive Directors, to folks who have taught from our platform, the leadership of Mount Hermon has always understood the words found in the Book of James 5:16:

> "The effectual, fervent prayer of a righteous man avails much."

But it is equally as important to know that prayer has been a vital concern for many people at Mount Hermon, beyond our leadership. Staff, counselors, and our guests have all experienced the power of prayer while on our campus. A few examples:

———— • • • ————

The first thing you noticed when you glanced at Steve was his size. He was a big man. Not fat. Big. He wasn't a bodybuilder, but you could easily tell his strength was beyond that of an average man. His T-shirt sleeves bulged every time he lifted one of his arms. His waist was thin, in contrast to his broad shoulders. At six feet, four inches tall, he clearly stood out. This guy was tough. His hair was closely cropped, giving the impression that Steve might be a military man, which was a good guess, a close guess, but not correct. Steve was a policeman.

Esther was Steve's wife, a small woman with dark hair and smiling eyes, who looked even more petite as she walked alongside her hulk of a husband. As tiny as she was, she made up for it with a large Bible she carried to every session. Esther had been faithfully attending our Mount Hermon conferences for several years, so I recognized her right off. But this was Steve's first visit, a full week of family camp during the summer of 2007.

I watched these two from a distance throughout the week. The body language seemed to be saying that Esther knew the Lord and was having a wonderful time here at Mount Hermon. I was getting a totally opposite vibe from Steve. As I watched them in the meetings—they always sat in the very back center section of the auditorium. Steve would do his best to pay attention, but he always seemed uncomfortable.

"I need you to help me pray that prayer."

On Thursday night, I was hosting our evening meeting. The music brought us into worship, and the speaker that evening included a powerful presentation of the Gospel. He closed in prayer, which was my cue to come back on stage to dismiss everyone. It was such a powerful moment. I felt that I couldn't let it go by without inviting anyone who had never accepted the Lord Jesus as personal Savior to do so. I quietly explained the Gospel one more time, asked everyone to bow their heads and told them to pray to the Lord, receiving His free gift of eternal life.

I finished with a prayer of my own. After saying "Amen," I opened my eyes, dismissed everyone, and began walking off the platform. Someone in the back center section of the auditorium caught my eye. It was Steve. He was still seated, right next to Esther, who appeared to be weeping. Steve motioned me back to where they were sitting.

I slipped into the row of seats in front of their row, and sat down. Steve looked at me with a piercing glance and simply uttered, "I need your help."

"How can I assist you?"

His answer was the kind that makes the ministry of Mount Hermon so worthwhile. "I need you to help me pray that prayer," he replied, gesturing up to the front of the auditorium.

I nodded. "You want help in praying a prayer to receive the Lord Jesus as your Savior?" I asked.

"Yeah," he answered. "That one."

Esther, who had been looking down the entire time, finally glanced at me with the largest smile I had ever seen. Her eyes were still welled up with tears, but now I understood they were tears of joy.

What a privilege, what a delight to walk Steve through a simple prayer of faith that night in the back of the auditorium. Because of that prayer, he was born into the family of God, passed from death unto life, forgiven of all his sins. He certainly heard from Heaven.

———— • • • ————

Kevin knows the power of prayer, too. He, his wife, Barbi, and their four kids attended our family camps since the early 1980s. "Our kids have grown up here!" he exclaimed, recounting all manner of tales about swimming, row boats, shuffleboard, and lots and lots of ice cream at the Fountain every evening.

But in the early 90s, the wheels fell off of Kevin and Barbi's marriage and divorce ultimately followed. It was devastating, as something of that magnitude always is to a family, but somehow Kevin saw his way clear to continue returning to Mount Hermon every summer, bringing the kids with him, even though he was now

"We have paused all along the way to hear from Heaven and the Lord has never disappointed us with His response."

officially a single parent. "I thought I'd be made to feel like a fifth wheel," he recounted, "but it was just the opposite—it was a real healing experience for all of us."

"Family Camp still works," he recalls as he thinks back on those days. "In some ways, it was even more meaningful to a single parent family than it may be to a family with Mom and Dad still under one roof. I will always be grateful for the teaching I received—especially from Ken and Mari Harrower who always made it a point to see how I was doing. They have a real heart for the hurting."

But for Kevin, the climactic event in his Mount Hermon visits occurred on a Friday afternoon several years after his divorce had finalized. The kids were off with their friends, so he had a rare few moments to himself. Kevin wandered over to the Chapel to enjoy the quiet, to reflect, and to pray. As he walked in, the sun was shining through the front windows. The stained glass windows on the lower half of the front wall displayed a field of wheat, creating an effect of holiness and peace.

"I went all the way up to the front pew," Kevin remembers, "and sat down quietly. As I sat there, I began to cry. I was so sad about how my family life was no more the picture-perfect little world I had imagined it had been all those years previously. But it was then that I realized God was asking of me what He had been asking of me all my life:

Kevin, can you trust Me? Am I really all you need in your life? Are you willing to live the rest of your life single if that is My will for you?"

Inside the Prayer Chapel

"That was it," Kevin recalls. "God had been allowing all these things to happen in my life in order to see if HE was enough for me. So right there, in the quietness of that Chapel, I prayed, telling the Lord He was all I needed and surrendering myself completely to Him once again. It was a powerful prayer.

"I realized there was a huge battle going on inside of me and the battle was all about 'Who is in *control*?' For me, it was a case described by the well-worn adage, 'Let go and let God.' I needed to give Him the driver's seat in the car of my life."

That afternoon, in our little Chapel, Kevin *prayed a prayer* that would make a huge difference in his life, and in the life of his family.

"I recently returned to Mount Hermon," Kevin relates, "with my children and my grandchildren accompanying me," and then he smiles, "and a wonderful new wife that God has blessed me with.

"While I was on the grounds, I once again stole off to the Chapel to offer a different prayer to the Lord. This time I prayed a prayer of *thanksgiving*, expressing my gratitude for how He has guided me through those rough days and showered me with the new blessings. What a wonderful way to pray—thank You, dear Lord!"

———— • • • ————

Stories like these are many and varied at Mount Hermon. Just come to one of our Victory Circle testimony meetings some Friday night in the summer if you don't believe me. The point is, Mount Hermon is inseparably linked with prayer. We've come through these one hundred-plus years due to God's faithful answers to our humble requests. We have paused all along the way to hear from Heaven and the Lord has never disappointed us with His response.

He answers prayers in places other than Mount Hermon, as well, so please don't misunderstand what I've said. There's nothing out of the ordinary about us in that respect. But I hope you have seen through these various snapshots of our history that God has built this ministry upon the foundation of the prayers of His people. And that is our hope for the future.

Will you join us? Will you commit to pray for Mount Hermon as often as we come to your mind? What a gift that would be to us! What a privilege to pray and then hear from Heaven.

✳

ACKNOWLEDGMENTS

THOSE OF YOU WHO KNOW ME KNOW THAT ONE OF MY FAVORITE WAYS TO RELAX IS TO SIT BY MY WIFE'S SIDE AND ENJOY A BASEBALL GAME PLAYED BY OUR BELOVED SAN FRANCISCO GIANTS. Rach and I have many glorious memories of munching on popcorn, sipping on iced tea and cheering loudly while sitting on the couch in front of our television. I'm far from a baseball expert, but I know enough to tell you this—it takes an entire team to win a baseball game. Pitching, fielding, hitting, base-running—all aspects strengthened by different members of the ball club—all put together for a winning season. It's that way with any team sport you can name.

It's the same way with a book, too, and this book is no exception. This is the work of a team. Even though it's my name on the front cover, I have many people to thank for their valuable contributions to these words that unfold on the previous pages.

It was my dear friend, Bill Butterworth who sat in my office with me in the spring of 2011 and offered to help me put together an updated story of Mount Hermon, along with my own story on paper. There have been two previous histories of Mount Hermon written. The first is entitled *Apart With Him*, written by Harry R.

Smith, which came out in 1956. Then, in 1972, *Rings in the Redwoods: The Story of Mount Hermon* by Kay Gudnason was an even more thorough and updated addition. I thank both of these authors for their invaluable assistance in chronicling the early history of Mount Hermon. Since both of these editions pre-dated my time here at Mount Hermon, I thought I could add to the story with some of the amazing accounts God caused to occur while I was serving here.

I am grateful indeed to all the folks who are mentioned in this book who gave of their time to be interviewed so the story could be told. Offer a prayer of thanksgiving for each name that is mentioned. They are precious folks to God, to Mount Hermon and to me.

Many of our own in-house Mount Hermon folks contributed to the finished product that you hold in your hands. Lisa Olson guided this book through its many final stages, for which I am so very grateful. Thanks also to Murphy Felton for overseeing Production and Josh Bootz as Designer. Alden Johanson did some important fact-checking for me. My friend, Camille Franicevich was an early reader and I am grateful for her feedback. Karen O'Connor graciously poured over the manuscript, making important editorial corrections and suggestions.

My entire Direct Report Group, affectionately known as the DRG, have tirelessly supported me in any project I have ever proposed, including the writing of this book. Deep gratitude is in order to Alden Johanson, Lisa Olson, Bill Fernald, Don Broesamle, Carrie Luther, Nate Pfefferkorn and J.R. Loofburrow.

Over the years, my personal assistant, Cindy Ritchie has put in hours and hours as a labor of love in order to help me in all manner of functions. This book would not have come to pass without her able assistance.

Mount Hermon's Board of Directors and Trustees are another two sources of enthusiastic encouragement and I want to thank each and every one of them for their support. I've been particularly close to the Board Chairmen over the years and so a special mention of Ron Singley and Rob Faisant is in order.

I want to express my gratitude to my two daughters and their families: Jeremy and Sara Bentley and their son, Dylan, and Nate and Joy Yetton and their son, Miles, have brought endless hours of delight to my life. We've all been through some major adventures together and I am eternally grateful to have this wonderful crew in my corner.

My wife Rachel is a helpmate in the fullest sense of the word. My partner here at Mount Hermon, my mate in life, she has painstakingly supported me through the years, in the good and the bad. I should also mention that she read through this manuscript with the watchful eye of an editor and her suggestions were greatly appreciated and used.

Last, and most significantly, I thank the Lord for allowing me to have played a small part in the furtherance of His Kingdom. That He would use one such as me is a testimony to His love and grace. Thank You, Lord, for Your touch on my life.

✳

ENDNOTES

ABOUT THE AUTHOR

PHOTOS
- Arriving at Mount Hermon in the early 1900s (Photograph).

- Dawson, D. (Photographer) 2011 *Roger & Rachel Williams* (Photograph).

- Bootz, J. (Photographer) 2013 *Roger Williams with a Roger Williams Bobble Head* (Photograph).

- Bootz, J. (Photographer) 2013 *Bill Butterworth and Roger Williams* (Photograph).

FOREWORD

PHOTOS
- Bootz, J. (Photographer) 2013 *Roger Williams with a Roger Williams Bobble Head* (Photograph).

- Bootz, J. (Photographer) 2013 *Bill Butterworth and Roger Williams* (Photograph).

CHAPTER 1

1. Roger Williams was hired under the title of Executive Director in 1993. The Executive Director title was changed to President/CEO in July 2013.

PHOTOS
- *Children in front of Newton Memorial* (Photograph).

- 1996 *Bruce Wilkenson* (Photograph).

- *Early Day Campers* (Photograph).

- Dawson, D. (Photographer) 1998 *Newton Memorial Construction* (Photograph).

- Dawson, D. (Photographer) 1998 *Kids in Day Camp in 1998* (Photograph).

CHAPTER 2

1. Gudnason, Kay, *Rings in the Redwoods: The Story of Mount Hermon.* (Mount Hermon, CA: Mount Hermon Association, Inc., 1972) p.1.

2. Ibid, p.2.

3. Smith, Harry R., *Apart With Him.* (Oakland, CA: Western Book and Tract Company, 1956) p.9.

4. Gudnason, Kay. *Rings in the Redwoods: The Story of Mount Hermon.* (Mount Hermon, CA: Mount Hermon Association, 1972.) p.5.

5. Ibid, p.5.

6. Ibid, p.6.

PHOTOS
- 1905 *Thornton Mills and Dr. Hugh W. Gilchrist at Glenwood* (Photograph).

- 1907 *Panoramic of Mount Hermon* (Photograph).

- 1905 *Stock Certificate* (Photograph).

- Guernsey , Lester C. (Photographer) *San Francisco 1906 earthquake Panoramic View* (Photograph) Library of Congress Panoramic collection (http://lcweb2.loc.gov/pp/panabt.html).

- 1905 *Founders* (Photograph).

CHAPTER 3

1. Gudnason, Kay. *Rings in the Redwoods: The Story of Mount Hermon.* (Mount Hermon, CA: Mount Hermon Association, 1972.) p.7.

2. Smith, Harry R. *Apart With Him.* (Oakland, CA: Western Book and Tract Company, 1956.) p.34.

3. Ibid, pp.45-46.

4. Ibid, p.46.

PHOTOS
- 1923 *Victory Circle Campfire* (Photograph).

- Dr. R. A. Torrey (Photograph).

- *Victory Circle* (Photograph).

CHAPTER 4

1. Gudnason, Kay. *Rings in the Redwoods: The Story of Mount Hermon.* (Mount Hermon, CA: The Mount Hermon Association, 1972.) p.328.

2. Ibid., p.331.

3. Ibid, p.106.

4. Ibid, p.106.

5. Ibid, p.106.

PHOTOS
- *Session in the Auditorium* (Photograph).

- *Young People's Conference* (Photograph).

- *Dr. Richard Halverson* (Photograph).

- *Mr. and Mrs. Robert Boyd Munger* (Photograph).

CHAPTER 5

1. Smith, Harry R., *Apart With Him.* (Oakland, CA: Western Book and Tract Company, 1956) p.86.

2. Ibid, p.86.

3. Simon, Stephanie., *Memorializing a Painful Chapter of History* (Wall Street Journal, August 20, 2011,) p.A4.

4. Smith, Harry R., *Apart With Him.* (Oakland, CA: Western Book and Tract Company, 1956) p.102.

5. Gudnason, Kay. *Rings in the Redwoods: The Story of Mount Hermon.* (Mount Hermon, CA: The Mount Hermon Association, 1972.) p.433.

6. Felton, Murphy. *Guest Group Global Impact* (Mount Hermon LOG. May–October 2011,) p.11.

PHOTOS
- *JEMs Conference 60th Anniversary Group Photo* (Photograph).

- *Director Ed Hayes with JEMs Leadership* (Photograph).

CHAPTER 6
1. Gudnason, Kay. *Rings in the Redwoods: The Story of Mount Hermon.* (Mount Hermon, CA: Mount Hermon Association, 1972.) p.364.

PHOTOS
- *Billy Graham, Jim and Bud Kennedy, Bill and Colette Gwinn touring Mount Hermon* (Photograph).

- *Gwinn shakes hands with Graham* (Photograph).

- *Graham visits Mount Hermon* (Photograph).

CHAPTER 7
1. Gudnason, Kay, *Rings in the Redwoods: The Story of Mount Hermon.* (Mount Hermon, CA: Mount Hermon Association, Inc., 1972) p.137.

2. Gwinn, Jim. *A Life Well Lived.* (Seattle, WA: CRISTA Ministries, 2005) p.4.

3. Ibid., p.5.

4. Ibid., p.6.

5. Gudnason, Kay, *Rings in the Redwoods: The Story of Mount Hermon.* (Mount Hermon, CA: Mount Hermon Association, Inc., 1972) p.138.

6. The Valley Press, Editorial,February 26, 1969.

7. Gwinn, Jim. A Life Well Lived. (Seattle, WA: CRISTA Ministries, 2005) p.7.

PHOTOS
- *Conference Drive 1950s* (Photograph).

- *Conference Drive 1930s* (Photograph).

- *Conference Drive 1940s* (Photograph).

- *Conference Drive 1950s* (Photograph).

- 1969 *Mount Hermon Road Slide* (Photograph).

- *Ed Hayes and Planning Committee* (Photograph).

CHAPTER 8

PHOTOS
- *Williams Family at Gull Lake Bible Conference* (Photograph).

- *Roger and Rachel with Sara, just before they accepted the call to Camp Barakel* (Photograph).

CHAPTER 9

PHOTOS
- Dawson, D. (Photographer) 1993 *Roger Williams at his desk* (Photograph).

CHAPTER 10

PHOTOS
- Kern, D. (Photographer) 2010 *Train leaving Redwood Camp* (Photograph).

- Dawson, D. (Photographer) 1993 *Rick Oliver* (Photograph).

CHAPTER 11

PHOTOS

- Velasquez, M. (Photographer) 2013 *Roger and Rachel Williams teaching at the Creating a Legacy Conference* (Photograph).

- Franicevich, J. (Photographer) *Bob & Camille Franicevich and Rachel & Roger Williams* (Photograph).

CHAPTER 12

PHOTOS

- Mendoza, C. (Photographer) 2011 *Clock Inscription* (Photograph).

- Mendoza, C. (Photographer) 2011 *Chapel Clock* (Photograph).

CHAPTER 13

PHOTOS

- 2003 *Centennial Banquet* (Photograph).

CHAPTER 14

PHOTOS

- Anderson, S. (Photographer) 2012 *Horse Pasture at Kidder Creek* (Photograph).

- 2012 *Whisper Canyon* (Photograph).

- Anderson, S. (Photographer) 2014 *Rafting the Kalamath River* (Photograph).

CHAPTER 15

PHOTOS

- Valesquez, M. (Photographer) 2013 *Praying with Great-Grandma* (Photograph).

- Dawson, D. (Photographer) 2010 *Prayer Chapel* (Photograph).